# New Junior Cycle

# Spanish Common Level



## Contents



### AUDIO INSTRUCTIONS

**The SEC 2022 Exam Paper, SEC Sample Paper and Edco Sample Paper audio tracks supplied on the Edco Audio App** reflect the examination, including all repeats, pauses and the number of times a track will be heard.

**The Edco Sample Paper audio tracks supplied on the Teacher's CD** are played only once.

### Audio Files Online

Enter the following code

biqrfg

on **www.e-xamit.ie** to view the aural exam scripts and play audio files online.

# Welcome to Spanish at Junior Cycle

Guide to Better Grades

Common Level

 **Marks:** 360

 **Time allowed:** 2 hours

In the following pages, you will find a very useful revision pack, containing everything you need to know for success throughout the year and in your exams. In the pack, you will find a course description of Junior Cycle Spanish, detailed exam paper analysis, sample questions and answers, key grammar points, vocabulary lists and key phrases, not just for the written exam, but for your entire Junior Cycle course.

Let's look at how you are assessed over the course of Junior Cycle Spanish.

- Two classroom-based assessments or CBAs.
- An assessment task (based on CBA2) to be completed in the classroom. The Assessment task is worth 10% of your marks.
- A final written exam. This exam is worth 90% and is at common level, meaning there are no Higher or Ordinary Levels.

The following sections will explore these in more detail, giving you tips, sample answers and the key vocabulary you need for success!

## Section 1: Course work

### 1. Classroom Based Assessment 1 (CBA1)

CBA1 is an oral test where you will have had an opportunity to show off your knowledge of Spanish. Perhaps you did a presentation on a holiday or favourite food or a role-play where you are shopping in a Spanish clothes shop or eating at a tapas bar. CBA1 should be completed by the end of second year and is organised by your teacher in the classroom.

### 2. Classroom Based Assessment 2 (CBA2)

CBA2 involves the completion of what is called *The Student Language Portfolio* and is completed around Christmas of Third Year. For CBA2 you must look back over the range of your work that you have completed and choose three pieces to be presented for assessment. You might have created material in various formats such as blogs, emails, letters, audio recordings, video recordings, cartoons, projects, poems, diary entries or stories. Remember you may present written, audio or digital texts as part of your *Student Language Portfolio*. The three pieces you select must include one in oral format and one which shows awareness of the culture of the Spanish-speaking world. Choose your three pieces carefully as this portfolio of your work will be the basis of your Assessment Task. When you look at the range of texts you have worked on, you should see the amazing ways you have developed in learning Spanish! This will really boost your confidence for *The Assessment Task* and the written exam.

### 3. The Assessment Task

The Assessment Task is worth 10% of your overall grade. This will take place after CBA2. It is based on the portfolio you presented for CBA2. Like the rest of the exam, it is Common Level. The Assessment Task has two stages and requires 80 minutes in total. This might be two single 40 minute classes. The first 40 minutes of the Assessment Task is for preparation. You will read, watch or listen to stimulus material and then discuss it in pairs, or groups, or with your class. You will then read the questions in the answer booklet provided by the State Examinations Commission, reflect on your experience of learning Spanish and think about how you might answer the questions. The second 40 minutes is for writing up your response. You will complete the answer booklet in English.

## Section 2: The Written Exam

### Breakdown

The written exam contains three sections and is worth 360 marks overall, or 90%. (Remember, the other 10% is for the Assessment Task) The marks awarded to each area are as follows:

| Section | |
|---|---|
| A Listening | 140 marks (35%) |
| B Reading | 140 marks (35%) |
| C Writing | 80 marks (20%) |

¡Hola! soy pan hasta la madre el trabajo el estudiante español saludos muy los gastos Carmen

When you are attempting some of the practice questions in these exam papers, use the vocabulary in this guide and your notes. Remember the more you do this, the more you will remember the vocabulary. You don't need to know it all straight away. The next section looks at the written paper, what type of questions to expect and how you should manage your timing.

### Timing of each section

- ✓ The listening section of your exam, Section A, will take about 30 minutes.
- ✓ Allow 45 minutes for the reading section.
- ✓ Don't spend too much time on the short questions such as matching and multiple choice. Instead, leave most of your time for the longer comprehension questions.
- ✓ The written section contains three questions. Allow 45 minutes for this section. Use most of the time for the longer questions where you produce your own written text, such as filling in a form or writing an email, blog, letter or diary entry.
- ✓ When you get your exam paper, take a moment and remember everything you have prepared.
- ✓ Note the timing, check the questions, make some notes of what vocabulary and phrases you could use for each question.
- ✓ Have a pen in your hand as you read.
- ✓ Brainstorm vocabulary and ideas that you think would suit the questions asked. In this way, you are actively working on the paper instead of simply reading it.
- ✓ Look at the pictures. What do you notice immediately? There are clues in there to help you with your answer.
- ✓ Attempt each question. There is more chance of getting marks for an attempt rather than leaving a blank space.

## Section A Listening

The listening section is worth 35% of your final grade. Each listening piece is played three times. Make sure to listen to Spanish as part of your revision – listen to tracks from past papers or textbooks. Is there anything you can prepare in advance? For example, if a question requires a day of the week, letters or numbers as an answer can you list them out in your rough work?

The listening section lasts about 30 minutes. Questions include: multiple choice picture-based questions; putting information in the correct order, as you hear it; and filling in a table based on information you have heard.

### Tips for Success:

Read the question carefully – do you need to answer in Spanish or English?

- ✓ Don't leave gaps – it is always best to attempt an answer.
- ✓ Don't tick more than one in the case of multiple choice.
- ✓ If you can only identify a word – write it in, you may even get some marks!
- ✓ If you aren't sure of the answer – what other answers have you got? Can you identify the missing one? Read the questions and answers carefully – what would make sense for the missing one?
- ✓ Practice listening to the whole listening piece, rather than just focusing on the questions. This will give you the "flow" of the conversation and the story of what you are hearing.
- ✓ If you are unsure of how many noughts there are in a million, thousand, etc, remember, you can write these large numbers in words.
- ✓ Make sure to use your rough work paper for brainstorming: keep your answer paper neat so that your initial answers are perfectly clear.
- ✓ Remember to write neatly in back or blue pen! Pencil fades on the paper.
- ✓ Be careful to answer each question according to the instructions. There are many different styles of question so you could be asked to answer in Spanish or in English, you might have to fill in a grid, to say whether a statement is true or false or to tick the correct answer in multiple choice questions.

## Section B: Reading

There are a variety of texts in the reading section. Texts might include matching images to Spanish words, descriptions or phrases, reading tweets, reviews or opinions, identifying information in texts such as a posters, flyers, menus or timetables and reading longer texts such as blogs, e-mails or journalistic articles. Be careful to answer in the correct language. Questions in Spanish should be answered in Spanish. Questions in English should be answered in English. Some of these questions may be multiple choice.

### Tips for Success

- Remember the questions will be in chronological order, so the answer to the first question will be located first in the text and so on.
- For match up exercises, match the ones you definitely know first. This will lessen the number of options remaining to complete the match up.
- For longer texts, focus on the sentences and phrases you understand. Can you piece them together to make a little mini-story of the longer text? Can you piece together the 'sense' of the text from this? Look at any pictures or headings for clues.
- In longer texts the question will often indicate which paragraph the answer is in. Make sure you take your answers from the correct paragraph.
- Check the number of answers required. Does the question ask you for two pieces of information, or three? Look at how many lines are provided for the answers and if they are numbered.
- Try not to leave anything blank. If you are really unsure of an answer, make an educated guess.

## Section C Writing

This section will be split into three questions. All questions should be answered in Spanish. The first written question will be a short question, such as completing sentences from a bank of phrases. The second and third questions will be longer pieces, such as writing a blog or responding to an email. The topics you have to write about will always be of relevance to your life, for example, you might have to write about your family, your hobbies, your holidays, your school or where you live.

## Key tips for success

- Don't forget all the work you have done previous to this exam! Have a look again at the corrections to your written work made by your teacher. Make a note of these and revise the points you need to.
- Read the instructions carefully and always plan your answers before you write.
- Do some rough work to brainstorm ideas and key verbs or vocabulary. This will help you link the parts together to make full sentences. Keep your sentences short and to the point.
- Make sure you are answering in the correct tense – should you be writing in the past, present or future? Check each point carefully!
- Pay attention to the structure of your work. It needs to be readable in order to get marks. If you are writing a longer text, such as a blog, divide your work into paragraphs and use black or blue pen in your writing.
- Always check back over your written work when you finish writing. Look at your verb endings, articles, the gender of nouns and adjective agreements. Check your work for spellings, punctuation and accents.
- Good handwriting will make a good impression, so be as neat and as accurate as you can.
- Writing simple sentences in accurate Spanish will get you good results !

Look at the following sample answers:

### Short answer question: Edco Sample Paper A, Section C, Question 16

Each part of this question has a choice of answers. Remember to complete the sentences you know first to eliminate the ones you are sure of. Look at the meaning of the sentence AND the grammar of the sentence, for example, in the sentences below, sentence (e) is clearly missing a verb, so the answer couldn't be '*de la mañana*' or '*al final de la calle*'. Look carefully at the possible answers you can choose from – '*para venir al instituto*' shows you that *para* is followed by an infinitive, this narrows down the options for the answer to sentence (a).

**Question 15**

Complete the following sentences by inserting the correct **Spanish** phrase into the space below:

**For example:**

Fui a España de vacaciones ***el verano pasado***.

**suelo llevar** **de la mañana**

**al final de la calle** **voy a visitar**

**mandar correos electrónicos** **para venir al instituto**

(a) Uso internet para **mandar correos electrónicos**.

(b) Me levanto a las siete **de la mañana**.

(c) El cine está **al final de la calle**.

(d) Cuando está lloviendo **suelo llevar** un impermeable.

(e) Este fin de semana **voy a visitar** a mi tía.

(f) Cojo el metro **para venir al instituto**.

### Long answer question: Edco Sample Paper A, Section C, Question 17

You are staying with a Spanish family in Madrid. Write a blog **in Spanish**, giving answers to the following:

(a) ¿Dónde vive la familia exactamente?

(b) ¿Qué te gusta más de Madrid?

(c) ¿Visitaste muchos sitios interesantes?

(d) ¿Tienes un nuevo amigo en Madrid?

(e) ¿Qué vas a hacer el fin de semana que viene?

This long answer question requires you to write a blog that includes the answers to FIVE different questions. Note how the sample answer is divided into five paragraphs, making it very clear to the examiner that each question has been answered. Note the length of each point – just three to four sentences per point is enough to get you full marks if your grammar and vocabulary are accurate, and you stick to the question that is asked.

**Mi Blog**

Me encanta la vida aquí en Madrid. Estoy de intercambio aquí con una familia española. La familia vive en un piso bastante grande en el centro de la ciudad. Todo está muy cerca y hay una parada de Metro al lado del piso.

Lo que más me gusta de Madrid son las tiendas. Me encanta la moda y voy de compras cada fin de semana. Hay de todo. Quiero comprar unos vaqueros este fin de semana.

El sábado pasado por la mañana fui al museo del Prado y al Palacio Real. ¡Por desgracia no vi a la Familia Real allí! El domingo pasado fui al parque del Retiro y pasé horas allí descansando y tomando el sol.

Tengo una nueva amiga aquí. Conocí a una chica muy simpática en el instituto. Se llama María. Es muy amable y me ayuda mucho cuando no entiendo a los profesores. Tenemos muchas cosas en común.

El viernes que viene voy a ir a una fiesta en la casa de María. Es el cumpleaños de su hermana Ana. Voy a llevar una tarta de chocolate y unos refrescos. El sábado voy a hacer una excursión a Salamanca con mi clase de español.

## Section 3: Grammar

In order to maximise your marks in written work, it is important to have good grammar. This section gives you revision notes to study the following grammar points:

A. Present tenses

B. Past tenses

C. Future tenses

D. Adjectives

E. Interrogatives

F. Articles

G. Important verbs

## A. Present tense

**The simple present tense.**

**Regular Verbs:**

To form the present tense of regular verbs, first drop the –ar, -er or –ir from the end of the infinitive. Then add the correct ending as shown in the table below.

| **Subject pronoun** | **-AR endings** | **HABLAR** | **-ER endings** | **COMER** | **-IR endings** | **VIVIR** |
|---|---|---|---|---|---|---|
| **Yo** (I) | **-o** | habl**o** | **-o** | com**o** | **-o** | viv**o** |
| **Tú** (you) | **-as** | habl**as** | **-es** | com**es** | **-es** | viv**es** |
| **Él/ella** (he/she) | **-a** | habl**a** | **-e** | com**e** | **-e** | viv**e** |
| **Nosotros/as** (we) | **-amos** | habl**amos** | **-emos** | com**emos** | **-imos** | viv**imos** |
| **Vosotros/as** (you plural) | **-áis** | habl**áis** | **-éis** | com**éis** | **-ís** | viv**ís** |
| **Ellos/ellas** (they) | **-an** | habl**an** | **-en** | com**en** | **-en** | viv**en** |

**Reflexive Verbs:**

These verbs are formed with the same endings as above, but have a reflexive pronoun before the verb.

| **Reflexive Pronoun** | **LAVARSE** | **To wash oneself** |
|---|---|---|
| Me (myself) | Yo **me** lavo | I wash myself |
| Te (yourself) | Tú **te** lavas | you wash yourself |
| Se (himself) | Él **se** lava | he washes himself |
| Se (herself) | Ella **se** lava | she washes herself |
| Nos (ourselves) | Nosotros **nos** lavamos | we wash ourselves |
| Os (yourselves) | Vosotros **os** laváis | you (plural) wash yourselves |
| Se (themselves) | Ellos **se** lavan | they wash themselves |
| Se (themselves) | Ellas **se** lavan | they (feminine) wash themselves |

**Irregular Verbs:**

These verbs do not follow any of the patterns shown above so they must be learned off by heart

| **SER (to be)** | **ESTAR (to be)** | **IR (to go)** | **HACER (to do)** | **DAR (to give)** | **SALIR (to go out)** |
|---|---|---|---|---|---|
| soy | estoy | voy | ha**go** | doy | sal**go** |
| eres | estás | vas | haces | das | sales |
| es | está | va | hace | da | sale |
| somos | estamos | vamos | hacemos | damos | salimos |
| sois | estáis | vais | hacéis | dais | salís |
| son | están | van | hacen | dan | salen |

| **TENER (to have)** | **VENIR (to come)** | **DECIR (to say)** | **VER (to see)** | **SABER (to know)** | **PONER (to put)** |
|---|---|---|---|---|---|
| ten**go** | ven**go** | di**go** | veo | sé | pon**go** |
| tienes | vienes | dices | ves | sabes | pones |
| tiene | viene | dice | ve | sabe | pone |
| tenemos | venimos | decimos | vemos | sabemos | ponemos |
| tenéis | venís | decís | veis | sabéis | ponéis |
| tienen | vienen | dicen | ven | saben | ponen |

**Radical Changing Verbs**

Radical changing verbs have a vowel change in all parts of the verb except *nosotros* (we) and *vosotros* (you plural) parts of the verb. The vowel might change from **e** to **ie**, **o** to **ue** or **u** to **ue** in the case of the verb *jugar*.

| QUERER (to like/want) | PODER (to be able to) | JUGAR (to play) |
|---|---|---|
| qu**ie**ro | p**ue**do | j**ue**go |
| qu**ie**res | p**ue**des | j**ue**gas |
| qu**ie**re | p**ue**de | j**ue**ga |
| queremos | podemos | jugamos |
| queréis | podéis | jugáis |
| qu**ie**ren | p**ue**den | j**ue**gan |

| | | | | | |
|---|---|---|---|---|---|
| (e-ie) | cerrar to close | | (o-ue) | volver | to return |
| | comenzar | to start | | costar | to cost |
| | despertar | to awaken | | encontrar | to meet |
| | preferir | to prefer | | poder | to be able to |
| | entender | to understand | | dormir | to sleep |
| | empezar | to start | | morir | to die |
| | querer | to want | | | |
| | pensar | to think | | | |
| | perder | to lose | | | |

**The present continuous tense.**

The present continuous tense is formed with the present tense of *estar* and the gerund of the verb. In English, the gerund ends in *–ing*, for example working, eating, living. In Spanish, the gerund of *–ar* verbs ends in *–ando*, gerund of *–er* and *–ir* verbs ends in *–iendo*.

**The gerund**

| | | | |
|---|---|---|---|
| -AR verbs | ➔ | Remove the *–ar* and add | *-ando* |
| -ER verbs | ➔ | Remove the –er and add | *-iendo* |
| -IR verbs | ➔ | Remove the *–ir* and add | *-iendo* |

| **Infinitive** | **Gerund** |
|---|---|
| habl**ar** | habl**ando** (*speaking*) |
| com**er** | com**iendo** (*eating*) |
| viv**ir** | viv**iendo** (*living*) |

**Irregular gerunds**

| | | |
|---|---|---|
| leer | ➔ | leyendo (*reading*) |
| dormir | ➔ | durmiendo (*sleeping*) |

## B. Past tenses

**The preterite tense.**

The preterite tense is used to talk about completed actions in the past.

**Regular Verbs:**

To form the preterite tense of regular verbs, first drop the *–ar, -er* or *–ir* from the end of the infinitive, then add the correct endings:

| | **-AR** | **HABLAR** | **-ER/-IR** | **COMER** |
|---|---|---|---|---|
| **Yo** | **-é** | habl**é** | **-í** | com**í** |
| **Tu** | **-aste** | habl**aste** | **-iste** | com**iste** |
| **Él/ella** | **-ó** | habl**ó** | **-ió** | com**ió** |
| **Nosotros** | **-amos** | habl**amos** | **-imos** | com**imos** |
| **Vosotros** | **-asteis** | habl**asteis** | **-isteis** | com**isteis** |
| **Ellos/ellas** | **-aron** | habl**aron** | **-ieron** | com**ieron** |

**Reflexive Verbs:**

To conjugate reflexive verbs in the preterite tense, use the same endings as above, but remember to put the reflexive pronoun before the verb.

LAVARSE (to wash oneself)

| | |
|---|---|
| **me** lavé | I washed myself |
| **te** lavaste | you washed yourself |
| **se** lavó | he washed himself/she washed herself |
| **nos** lavamos | we washed ourselves |
| **os** lavasteis | you (plural) washed yourselves |
| **se** lavaron | they washed themselves |

**Radical Changing Verbs:**

Radical changing verbs ending in *–ar* and *–er* have a vowel change in the PRESENT tense, however, in the PAST tense there is no vowel change.

Radical changing verbs ending in *–ir* have a vowel change in the third and sixth persons of the preterite tense (for *él / ella / usted* and for *ellos / ellas / ustedes*).

PEDIR

pedí

pediste

p**i**dió

pedimos

pediste

p**i**dieron

**Verbs with irregular 'yo' forms in the preterite tense:**

BUSCAR – yo busqué

EMPEZAR – yo empecé

JUGAR – yo jugué

LLEGAR – yo llegué

TOCAR – yo toqué

SACAR – yo saqué

**Irregular Verbs:**

The following verbs are irregular in the preterite tense and should be learned off by heart

| **SER (to be)** | **IR (to go)** | **ESTAR (to be)** | **TENER (to have)** | **ANDAR (to walk)** |
|---|---|---|---|---|
| fui | fui | estuve | tuve | anduve |
| fuiste | fuiste | estuviste | tuviste | anduviste |
| fue | fue | estuvo | tuvo | anduvo |
| fuimos | fuimos | estuvimos | tuvimos | anduvimos |
| fuisteis | fuisteis | estuvisteis | tuvisteis | anduvisteis |
| fueron | fueron | estuvieron | tuvieron | anduvieron |

| **DAR (to give)** | **VER (to see)** | **HACER (to do)** | **QUERER (to want)** | **PONER (to put)** |
|---|---|---|---|---|
| di | vi | hice | quise | puse |
| diste | viste | hiciste | quisiste | pusiste |
| dio | vio | hi**z**o | quiso | puso |
| dimos | vimos | hicimos | quisimos | pusimos |
| disteis | visteis | hicisteis | quisisteis | pusisteis |
| dieron | vieron | hicieron | quisieron | pusieron |

| **DECIR (to say)** | **VENIR (to come)** |
|---|---|
| dije | vine |
| dijiste | viniste |
| dijo | vino |
| dijimos | vinimos |
| dijisteis | vinisteis |
| dijeron | vinieron |

## The imperfect tense.

The imperfect tense is used to talk about repeated actions in the past (things you 'used to' do). It is also used to describe actions that were in progress in the past (things you were doing) and it is used to describe feelings or emotions in the past or to describe anything that sets a scene.

**Regular Verbs:**

To form the imperfect tense of regular verbs, remove the *–ar, -er or –ir* and add the following endings:

| -AR VERBS | HABLAR | -ER and -IR verbs | VIVIR |
|---|---|---|---|
| -aba | hablaba | -ía | vivía |
| -abas | hablabas | -ías | vivías |
| -aba | hablaba | -ía | vivía |
| -ábamos | hablábamos | -íamos | vivíamos |
| -abais | hablabais | -íais | vivíais |
| -aban | hablaban | -ían | vivían |

**Irregular Verbs:**

There are just three verbs that are irregular in the imperfect:

| SER | IR | VER |
|---|---|---|
| era | iba | veía |
| eras | ibas | veías |
| era | iba | veía |
| éramos | íbamos | veíamos |
| erais | ibais | veíais |
| eran | iba | veían |

**Phrases that indicate the use of the imperfect:**

| | |
|---|---|
| siempre | always |
| con frecuencia | frequently |
| frecuentemente | frequently |
| a menudo | often |
| a veces | sometimes |
| de vez en cuando | from time to time |
| muchas veces | many times |
| cada año/cada mes | every year / every month |
| cada semana/cada día | every week / every day |
| todos los días | every day |
| cada lunes/cada martes... | every Monday / every Tuesday |

## The present perfect tense.

The present perfect tense is used to talk about things you have done. It is formed by using the present tense of the verb HABER and the past participle.

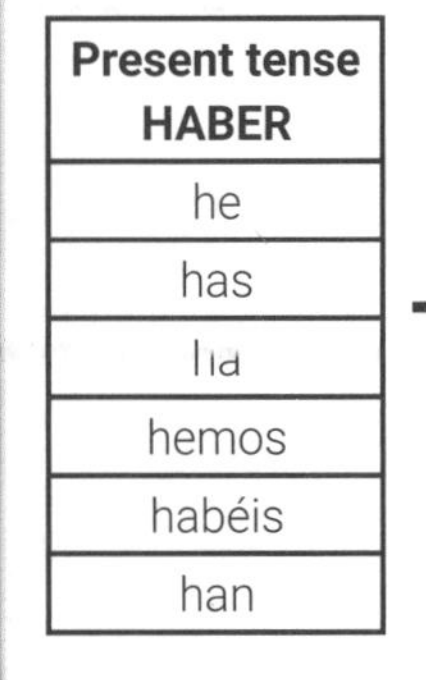

| Present tense HABER |
|---|
| he |
| has |
| ha |
| hemos |
| habéis |
| han |

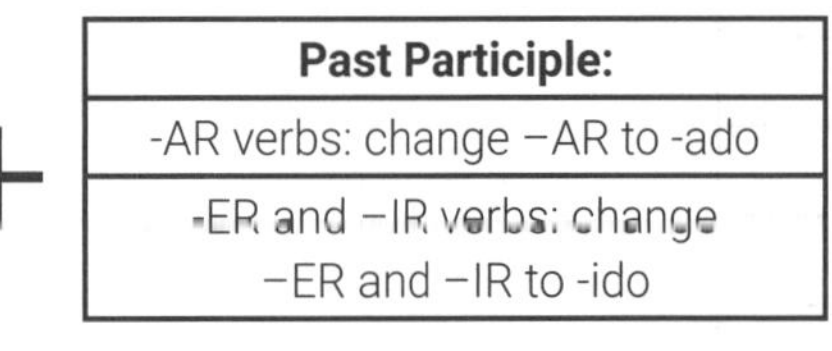

+

| Past Participle: |
|---|
| -AR verbs: change –AR to -ado |
| -ER and –IR verbs: change –ER and –IR to -ido |

For example:

*He comido la tortilla.* I have eaten the omellette.

*¿Has hablado con Maite?* Have you spoken to Maite?

*Han jugado el partido.* They've played the match.

**The following commonly used verbs have irregular past participles:**

| | | |
|---|---|---|
| ABRIR | abierto | opened |
| DECIR | dicho | said |
| ESCRIBIR | escrito | written |
| HACER | hecho | done |
| LEER | leído | read |
| MORIR | muerto | died |
| OÍR | oído | heard |
| PONER | puesto | put |
| ROMPER | roto | broken |
| VER | visto | seen |
| VOLVER | vuelto | returned |

| | |
|---|---|
| *Juan ha abierto la puerta.* | Juan has opened the door. |
| *Los niños han roto la ventana.* | The children have broken the window. |
| *He visto esta película.* | I have seen that film. |

## C. Future tenses

In Spanish (as in English) there are two future tenses, the 'going to' future and the 'will' future.

**The 'going to' future**

To form the 'going to' future we use the following structure

***Present tense of IR* + a + infinitive***

| | | |
|---|---|---|
| For example... | Voy a salir esta noche. | I am going to go out tonight. |
| | Vamos a ir a la discoteca. | We are going to go to the disco. |
| | Van a jugar al tenis. | They are going to play tennis. |
| | Juan va a llegar a las ocho. | Juan is going to arrive at 8:00. |

*Present tense of IR = voy, vas, va, vamos, vais, van

**The 'will' future**

The 'will' future tense is formed by adding the following endings to the infinitive *-é, ás, á, -emos, -éis, -án*. We use the same endings with all verbs, including –ar, -er, -ir verbs, radical changing verbs and reflexive verbs.

| | | | |
|---|---|---|---|
| hablar**é** | (I will speak) | comer**é** (i will eat) | vivir**é** (i will live) |
| hablar**ás** | (you will speak) | comer**ás** | vivir**ás** |
| hablar**á** | (he/she will speak) | comer**á** | vivir**á** |
| hablar**emos** | (we will speak) | comer**emos** | vivir**emos** |
| hablar**éis** | (you plural will speak) | comer**éis** | vivir**éis** |
| hablar**án** | (they will speak) | comer**án** | vivir**án** |

Examples :

| | |
|---|---|
| Llegaré a casa a las seis. | I will arrive at 6. |
| ¿Irás a España? | Will you go to Spain? |

**Useful expressions for the future:**

| | | | |
|---|---|---|---|
| mañana | *tomorrow* | el lunes que viene | *next Monday* |
| esta tarde | *this afternoon/evening* | la semana que viene | *next week* |
| esta noche | *tonight* | el verano que viene | *next summer* |
| el año que viene | *next year* | el fin de semana que viene | *next weekend* |

**ALL verbs form the 'will' future tense in this way apart from the following verbs, which have irregular stems (NOTE the endings are still the same!)**

| Infinitive | 'Yo' form | Full conjugation |
|---|---|---|
| DECIR (to say) | diré | diré, dirás, dirá, diremos, diréis, dirán |
| HABER (to have) | habré | habré, habrás, habrá, habremos, habréis, habrán |
| HACER (to make/do) | haré | haré, harás, hará, haremos, haréis, harán |
| PODER (to be able to) | podré | podré, podrás, podrá, podremos, podréis, podrán |
| PONER (to put) | pondré | pondré, pondrás, pondrá, pondremos, pondréis, pondrán |
| QUERER (to want) | querré | querré, querrás, querrá, querremos, querréis, querrán |
| SABER (to know) | sabré | sabré, sabrás, sabrá, sabremos, sabréis, sabrán |
| SALIR (to go out) | saldré | saldré, saldrás, saldrá, saldremos, saldréis, saldrán |
| TENER (to have) | tendré | tendré, tendrás, tendrá, tendremos, tendréis, tendrán |
| VENIR (to come) | vendré | vendré, vendrás, vendrá, vendremos, vendréis, vendrán |

## D. Adjectives

Adjectives are describing words. They are usually placed after the noun they describe but must always agree in number and gender with the noun or nouns they describe.

**Adjectives ending in –o in the masculine singular change their ending to –a in the feminine singular and to –os in the masculine plural and –as in the feminine plural.**

| | |
|---|---|
| el mercado modern**o** | los mercados modern**os** |
| la casa modern**a** | las casas modern**as** |

**Adjectives ending in consonants, -ista or –e have the same ending for both masculine and feminine. These adjectives add –s or –es to make them plural.**

| | |
|---|---|
| el chico popular | los chicos popular**es** |
| la chica popular | las chicas popular**es** |
| el campo grande | los campos grande**s** |
| la casa grande | las casas grande**s** |

**Adjectives ending in –or and adjectives of nationality add –a in the feminine. These adjectives add –es in the masculine plural and –as in the feminine plural.**

| | |
|---|---|
| Juan es hablador. | Juan y Ana son hablador**es**. |
| Ana es hablador**a**. | Ana y Sara son hablador**as**. |
| un español | unos español**es** |
| una español**a** | unas español**as** |

**The following adjectives are placed before the nouns and have a shortened form before masculine singular nouns.**

| | | |
|---|---|---|
| bueno | (good) | un buen chico |
| malo | (bad) | un mal chico |
| primero | (first) | el primer señor |
| tercero | (third) | el tercer libro |
| alguno | (some) | alg**ú**n dinero |
| ninguno | (none) | ning**ú**n dinero |

**Grande has a shortened form before both masculine and feminine singular nouns, but when used in this short form before the noun it means 'famous/great', after the noun it means 'big'.**

| | |
|---|---|
| un **gran** hombre | a great man |
| una g**ra**n mujer | a great woman |
| un hombre g**rande** | a big man |

**Possessive Adjectives agree with the nouns after them.**

Nuestr**a** cas**a** es muy grande.

Nuestr**os** abuel**os** viven en Londres.

**POSSESSIVE ADJECTIVES**

| | Masculine | feminine | masc. Plural | fem. Plural |
|---|---|---|---|---|
| My | mi | | mis | |
| Your | tu | | tus | |
| His | su | | sus | |
| Her | su | | sus | |
| Your (usted) | su | | sus | |
| Our | nuestro | nuestra | nuestros | nuestras |
| Your (plural) | vuestro | vuestra | vuestros | vuestras |
| Their | su | | sus | |
| Your (ustedes) | su | | sus | |

**Demonstrative Adjectives also agree with the nouns after them.**

est**os** libr**os** — these books
es**a** chic**a** — that girl

| | Masculine | Feminine |
|---|---|---|
| This | este | esta |
| These | estos | estas |
| That | ese | esa |
| Those | esos | esas |

## E. Interrogatives – question words

| | | | |
|---|---|---|---|
| **¿Qué?** | *What?* | ¿Qué hora es? | *What time is it?* |
| **¿Cómo?** | *How?* | ¿Cómo estás? | *How are you?* |
| **¿Cuándo?** | *When?* | ¿Cúando llegaste? | *When did you arrive?* |
| **¿Dónde?** | *Where?* | ¿Dónde vives? | *Where did you live?* |
| **¿Adónde?** | *To where?* | ¿Adónde vas? | *Where are you going?* |
| **¿Quién/es?** | *Who?* | ¿Quién es ese hombre? | *Who is that man?* |
| **¿Por qué?** | *Why?* | ¿Por qué no vienes? | *Why are you not coming?* |
| **¿Cuál/es?** | *Which?* | ¿Cuál prefieres? | *Which do you prefer?* |
| **¿Cuánto?** | *How much?* | ¿Cuánto cuesta? | *How much does it cost?* |

## F. Articles

**The definite article (*the*)**

In Spanish there are four ways to say 'the' – *el, la, los* and *las*. **El** is used before masculine nouns, **la** is used before feminine nouns, **los** is used before masculine plural nouns and **las** is used before feminine plural nouns.

**el** chico — the boy
**la** chica — the girl
**los** chicos — the boys
**las** chicas — the girls

**The indefinite article (a)**

There are two ways to say 'a' – *un* and *una*. **Un** is used before masculine nouns, **una** is used before feminine nouns. In the plural these become **unos** and **unas.**

**un** chico — a boy
**una** chica — a girl
**unos** chicos — some boys
**unas** chicas — some girls

## G. Important verbs

Here is a complete listing of the verbs you should know for Junior Cycle.

**AR VERBS**

BAILAR (to dance)

| Present | Present Continuous | Future |
|---|---|---|
| bailo | estoy bailando | bailaré |
| bailas | estás bailando | bailarás |
| baila | está bailando | bailará |
| bailamos | estamos bailando | bailaremos |
| bailáis | estáis bailando | bailaréis |
| bailan | están bailando | bailarán |
| **Preterite** | **Imperfect** | **Present Perfect** |
| bailé | bailaba | he bailado |
| bailaste | bailabas | has bailado |
| bailó | bailaba | ha bailado |
| bailamos | bailábamos | hemos bailado |
| bailasteis | bailabais | habéis bailado |
| bailaron | bailaban | han bailado |

**ER VERBS**

COMER (to eat)

| Present | Present Continuous | Future |
|---|---|---|
| como | estoy comiendo | comeré |
| comes | estás comiendo | comerás |
| come | está comiendo | comerá |
| comemos | estamos comiendo | comeremos |
| coméis | estáis comiendo | comeréis |
| comen | están comiendo | comerán |
| **Preterite** | **Imperfect** | **Present Perfect** |
| comí | comía | he comido |
| comiste | comías | has comido |
| comió | comía | ha comido |
| comimos | comíamos | hemos comido |
| comisteis | comíais | habéis comido |
| comieron | comían | han comido |

**-IR VERBS**

VIVIR (to live)

| Present | Present Continuous | Future |
|---|---|---|
| vivo | estoy viviendo | viviré |
| vives | estás viviendo | vivirás |
| vive | está viviendo | vivirá |
| vivimos | estamos viviendo | viviremos |
| vivís | estáis viviendo | viviréis |
| viven | están viviendo | vivirán |
| **Preterite** | **Imperfect** | **Present Perfect** |
| viví | vivía | he vivido |
| viviste | vivías | has vivido |
| vivió | vivía | ha vivido |
| vivimos | vivíamos | hemos vivido |
| vivisteis | vivíais | habéis vivido |
| vivieron | vivían | han vivido |

## IRREGULAR VERBS

| Infinitive | Present | Future |
|---|---|---|
| **DAR** to give | doy | daré |
| | das | darás |
| | da | dará |
| | damos | daremos |
| | dais | daréis |
| | dan | darán |
| **Preterite** | **Imperfect** | **Present Perfect** |
| di | daba | he dado |
| diste | dabas | has dado |
| dio | daba | ha dado |
| dimos | dábamos | hemos dado |
| disteis | dabais | habéis dado |
| dieron | daban | han dado |

| Infinitive | Present | Future |
|---|---|---|
| **DECIR** to say | digo | diré |
| | dices | darás |
| | dice | dará |
| | decimos | daremos |
| | decís | daréis |
| | dicen | darán |
| **Preterite** | **Imperfect** | **Present Perfect** |
| dije | decía | he dicho |
| dijiste | decías | has dicho |
| dijo | decía | ha dicho |
| dijimos | decíamos | hemos dicho |
| dijisteis | decíais | habéis dicho |
| dijeron | decían | han dicho |

| Infinitive | Present | Future |
|---|---|---|
| **ESTAR** to be | estoy | estaré |
| | estás | estarás |
| | está | estará |
| | estamos | estaremos |
| | estáis | estaréis |
| | están | estarán |
| **Preterite** | **Imperfect** | **Present Perfect** |
| estuve | estaba | he estado |
| estuviste | estabas | has estado |
| estuvo | estaba | ha estado |
| estuvimos | estábamos | hemos estado |
| estuvisteis | estabais | habéis estado |
| estuvieron | estaban | han estado |

| Infinitive | Present | Future |
|---|---|---|
| **HACER** to make/do | hago | haré |
| | haces | harás |
| | hace | hará |
| | hacemos | haremos |
| | hacéis | haréis |
| | hacen | harán |
| **Preterite** | **Imperfect** | **Present Perfect** |
| hice | hacía | he hecho |
| hiciste | hacías | has hecho |
| hizo | hacía | ha hecho |
| hicimos | hacíamos | hemos hecho |
| hicisteis | hacíais | habéis hecho |
| hicieron | hacían | han hecho |

| Infinitive | Present | Future |
|---|---|---|
| **IR** to go | voy | iré |
| | vas | irás |
| | va | irá |
| | vamos | iremos |
| | vais | iréis |
| | van | irán |
| **Preterite** | **Imperfect** | **Present Perfect** |
| fui | iba | he ido |
| fuiste | ibas | has ido |
| fue | iba | ha ido |
| fuimos | íbamos | hemos ido |
| fuisteis | ibais | habéis ido |
| fueron | iban | han ido |

| Infinitive | Present | Future |
|---|---|---|
| **JUGAR** to play | juego | jugaré |
| | juegas | jugarás |
| | juega | jugará |
| | jugamos | jugaremos |
| | jugáis | jugaréis |
| | juegan | jugarán |
| **Preterite** | **Imperfect** | **Present Perfect** |
| jugué | jugaba | he jugado |
| jugaste | jugabas | has jugado |
| jugó | jugaba | ha jugado |
| jugamos | jugábamos | hemos jugado |
| jugasteis | jugabais | habéis jugado |
| jugaron | jugaban | han jugado |

| Infinitive | Present | Future |
|---|---|---|
| **PODER** to be able to | puedo | podré |
| | puedes | podrás |
| | puede | podrá |
| | podemos | podremos |
| | podéis | podréis |
| | pueden | podrán |
| **Preterite** | **Imperfect** | **Present Perfect** |
| pude | podía | he podido |
| pudiste | podías | has podido |
| pudo | podía | ha podido |
| pudimos | podíamos | hemos podido |
| pudisteis | podíais | habéis podido |
| pudieron | podían | han podido |

| Infinitive | Present | Future |
|---|---|---|
| **PONER** to put | pongo | pondré |
| | pones | pondrás |
| | pone | pondrá |
| | ponemos | pondremos |
| | ponéis | pondréis |
| | ponen | pondrán |
| **Preterite** | **Imperfect** | **Present Perfect** |
| puse | ponía | he puesto |
| pusiste | ponías | has puesto |
| puso | ponía | ha puesto |
| pusimos | poníamos | hemos puesto |
| pusisteis | poníais | habéis puesto |
| pusieron | ponían | han puesto |

| Infinitive | Present | Future |
|---|---|---|
| **QUERER** to want/wish/ love | quiero | querré |
| | quieres | querrás |
| | quiere | querrá |
| | queremos | querremos |
| | queréis | querréis |
| | quieren | querrán |
| **Preterite** | **Imperfect** | **Present Perfect** |
| quise | quería | he querido |
| quisiste | querías | has querido |
| quiso | quería | ha querido |
| quisimos | queríamos | hemos querido |
| quisisteis | queríais | habéis querido |
| quisieron | querían | han querido |

| Infinitive | Present | Future |
|---|---|---|
| **SABER** to know | sé | sabré |
| | sabes | sabrás |
| | sabe | sabrá |
| | sabemos | sabremos |
| | sabéis | sabréis |
| | saben | sabrán |
| **Preterite** | **Imperfect** | **Present Perfect** |
| supe | sabía | he sabido |
| supiste | sabías | has sabido |
| supo | sabía | ha sabido |
| supimos | sabíamos | hemos sabido |
| supisteis | sabíais | habéis sabido |
| supieron | sabían | han sabido |

| Infinitive | Present | Future |
|---|---|---|
| **SALIR** to go out | salgo | saldré |
| | sales | saldrás |
| | sale | saldrá |
| | salimos | saldremos |
| | salís | saldréis |
| | salen | saldrán |
| **Preterite** | **Imperfect** | **Present Perfect** |
| salí | salía | he salido |
| saliste | salías | has salido |
| salió | salía | ha salido |
| salimos | salíamos | hemos salido |
| salisteis | salíais | habéis salido |
| salieron | salían | han salido |

| Infinitive | Present | Future |
|---|---|---|
| **SER** to be | soy | seré |
| | eres | serás |
| | es | será |
| | somos | seremos |
| | sois | seréis |
| | son | serán |
| **Preterite** | **Imperfect** | **Present Perfect** |
| fui | era | he sido |
| fuiste | eras | has sido |
| fue | era | ha sido |
| fuimos | éramos | hemos sido |
| fuisteis | erais | habéis sido |
| fueron | eran | han sido |

| Infinitive | Present | Future |
|---|---|---|
| **TENER** to have | tengo | tendré |
| | tienes | tendrás |
| | tiene | tendrá |
| | tenemos | tendremos |
| | tenéis | tendréis |
| | tienen | tendrán |
| **Preterite** | **Imperfect** | **Present Perfect** |
| tuve | tenía | he tenido |
| tuviste | tenías | has tenido |
| tuvo | tenía | ha tenido |
| tuvimos | teníamos | hemos tenido |
| tuvisteis | teníais | habéis tenido |
| tuvieron | tenían | han tenido |

| Infinitive | Present | Future |
|---|---|---|
| **VENIR** to come | vengo | vendré |
| | vienes | vendrás |
| | viene | vendrá |
| | venimos | vendremos |
| | venís | vendréis |
| | vienen | vendrán |
| **Preterite** | **Imperfect** | **Present Perfect** |
| vine | venía | he venido |
| viniste | venías | has venido |
| vino | venía | ha venido |
| vinimos | veníamos | hemos venido |
| vinisteis | veníais | habéis venido |
| vinieron | venían | han venido |

| Infinitive | Present | Future |
|---|---|---|
| **VER** to see | veo | veré |
| | ves | verás |
| | ve | verá |
| | vemos | veremos |
| | veis | veréis |
| | ven | verán |
| **Preterite** | **Imperfect** | **Present Perfect** |
| vi | veía | he visto |
| viste | veías | has visto |
| vio | veía | ha visto |
| vimos | veíamos | hemos visto |
| visteis | veíais | habéis visto |
| vieron | veían | han visto |

## Section 4: Key vocabulary

### Los números – Numbers

| | | | |
|---|---|---|---|
| 0 | cero | 28 | *veintiocho* |
| 1 | uno | 29 | *veintinueve* |
| 2 | dos | 30 | treinta |
| 3 | tres | 31 | treinta y uno/a |
| 4 | cuatro | 32 | treinta y dos |
| 5 | cinco | 40 | cuarenta |
| 6 | seis | 50 | cincuenta |
| 7 | siete | 60 | sesenta |
| 8 | ocho | 70 | setenta |
| 9 | nueve | 80 | ochenta |
| 10 | diez | 90 | noventa |
| 11 | once | 100 | cien |
| 12 | doce | 101 | ciento uno/a |
| 13 | trece | 111 | ciento once |
| 14 | catorce | 120 | ciento veinte |
| 15 | quince | 200 | doscientos/as |
| 16 | dieciséis | 300 | trescientos/as |
| 17 | diecisiete | 400 | cuatrocientos/as |
| 18 | dieciocho | 500 | **quinientos/as** |
| 19 | diecinueve | 600 | seiscientos/as |
| 20 | veinte | 700 | **setecientos/as** |
| 21 | *veintiuno/a* | 800 | ochocientos/as |
| 22 | *veintidós* | 900 | **novecientos/as** |
| 23 | *veintitrés* | 1000 | mil |
| 24 | *veinticuatro* | 2000 | dos mil |
| 25 | *veinticinco* | 2007 | dos mil siete |
| 26 | *veintiséis* | 1000000 | un millón |
| 27 | *veintisiete* | 2000000 | dos millones |

| | | | |
|---|---|---|---|
| 1st | primer/o/a | 6th | sexto/a |
| 2nd | segundo/a | 7th | séptimo/a |
| 3rd | tercer/o/a | 8th | octavo/a |
| 4th | cuarto/a | 9th | noveno/a |
| 5th | quinto/a | 10th | décimo/a |

| | | | |
|---|---|---|---|
| 1:00 | **es** la una | 5:30 | son las cinco y media |
| 2:00 | son las dos | 7:45 | son las ocho menos cuarto |
| 3:00 | son las tres | 10:35 | son las once menos veinticinco |
| 4:00 | son las cuatro | am | de la mañana |
| 6:15 | son las seis y cuarto | pm | de la tarde / de la noche |

**NOTES ON NUMBERS:**

***For numbers ending in 1 (21, 31, 41 etc), drop the –o before masculine nouns and change –o to –a before feminine nouns**

| | | |
|---|---|---|
| Example: | ¿Cuántos chicos hay en la clase?<br>- veintiu**no** | How many boys are in the class?<br>twenty-one |
| | Hay veinti**ún** chicos en la clase. | There are 21 boys in the class. |
| | Hay veinti**una** chicas en la clase. | There are 21 girls in the class. |

***Hundreds change –os /-as for masculine / feminine**

| | | |
|---|---|---|
| Example: | doscient**os** niños | 200 boys |
| | doscient**as** niñas | 200 girls |

***In dates NEVER TRANSLATE 'AND'**

Example: 2007 dos mil siete (<u>not</u> *dos mil y siete*)

***Primero and tercero shorten to primer and tercer before masculine singular nouns**

| | | |
|---|---|---|
| Example: | El 1º piso | = el **primer** piso |
| | La 1ª planta | = la primer**a** planta |
| | El 3º piso | = el **tercer** piso |
| | La 3ª planta | = la tercer**a** planta |

***Use regular numbers with dates**

Example: 02/03 = el **dos** de marzo

***Use full numbers with years**

Example: 1998 = mil novecientos noventa y ocho

***100 (ciento) is shortened to cien if it is followed by a noun (masculine or feminine)**

| | | |
|---|---|---|
| Example: | *cien* libros | 100 books |
| | *cien* plumas | 100 pens |
| | ciento dos | 102 |
| | ciento treinta | 130 |

**Los días de la semana – The days of the week**

| | |
|---|---|
| lunes | Monday |
| martes | Tuesday |
| miércoles | Wednesday |
| jueves | Thursday |
| viernes | Friday |
| sábado | Saturday |
| domingo | Sunday |

**Los meses del año – The months of the year**

| | |
|---|---|
| enero | January |
| febrero | February |
| marzo | March |
| abril | April |
| mayo | May |
| junio | June |
| julio | July |
| agosto | August |
| septiembre | September |
| octubre | October |
| noviembre | November |
| diciembre | December |

**Las estaciones – The seasons**

| | |
|---|---|
| la primavera | Spring |
| el verano | Summer |
| el otoño | Autumn |
| el invierno | Winter |

**La hora – Time**

| | |
|---|---|
| 1:00 | la una |
| 2:00 | las dos |
| 3:00 | las tres |
| 4:00 | las cuatro |
| 5:00 | las cinco |
| 6:05 | las seis y cinco |
| 7:10 | las siete y diez |
| 8:15 | las ocho y cuarto |
| 9:20 | las nueve y veinte |
| 10:25 | las diez y veinticinco |
| 11:35 | las doce menos veinticinco |
| 12:40 | la una menos veinte |
| 1:45 | las dos menos cuarto |
| 2:50 | las tres menos diez |
| 7:55 | las ocho menos cinco |

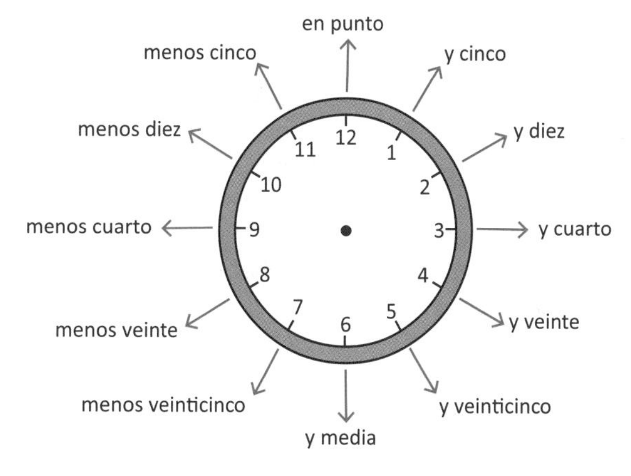


| | |
|---|---|
| de la mañana | am |
| de la tarde | pm |
| de la noche | pm |
| el mediodía | midday |
| la medianoche | midnight |

**La familia – The family**

| | |
|---|---|
| el padre | father |
| la madre | mother |
| los padres | parents |
| el hijo | son |
| la hija | daughter |
| los hijos | children |
| el hermano | brother |
| la hermana | sister |
| los hermanos | siblings |
| los gemelos | twins |
| el abuelo | grandfather |
| la abuela | grandmother |
| el primo | cousin (m) |
| la prima | cousin (f) |
| el tío | uncle |
| la tía | aunt |
| el nieto | grandson |
| la nieta | granddaughter |
| el sobrino | nephew |
| la sobrina | niece |
| el novio | boyfriend |
| la novia | girlfriend |
| el padrastro | step-father |
| la madrastra | step-mother |

**Los colores – Colours**

| | |
|---|---|
| rojo | red |
| naranja | orange |
| amarillo | yellow |
| verde | green |
| azul | blue |
| morado | purple |
| rosa | pink |
| blanco | white |
| negro | black |
| gris | grey |
| marrón | brown |

**Las profesiones – Jobs**

| | |
|---|---|
| el cajero / la cajera | cashier |
| el cocinero / la cocinera | cook / chef |
| el médico / la médica | doctor |
| el ingeniero / la ingeniera | engineer |
| el pescador / la pescadora | fisherman / fisherwoman |
| el mecánico / la mecánica | mechanic |
| el enfermero / la enfermera | nurse |
| el profesor / la profesora | teacher |
| el camarero / la camarera | waiter / waitress |
| el arquitecto / la arquitecta | architect |
| el granjero / la granjera | farmer |
| el abogado / la abogada | solicitor |
| el carnicero / la carnicera | butcher |
| el conductor / la conductora | driver |
| el bombero / la bombera | fireman |
| el periodista / la periodista | journalist |
| el dependiente / la dependienta | shop assistant |
| la azafata | air hostess |
| el auxiliar de vuelo | flight attendant |
| el farmacéutico / la farmacéutica | pharmacist |
| el peluquero / la peluquera | hairdresser |
| el marinero / la marinera | sailor |
| el maestro / la maestra | primary school teacher |
| el soldado / la soldado | soldier |
| el fontanero / la fontanera | plumber |
| el actor / la actriz | actor / actress |
| el contable / la contable | accountant |
| el socorrista / la socorrista | life guard |
| el veterinario / la veterinaria | vet |

**La casa – The house**

| | |
|---|---|
| arriba | upstairs |
| abajo | downstairs |
| la planta baja | the ground floor |
| la primera planta | the first floor |
| la segunda planta | the second floor |
| la tercera planta | the third floor |
| el sótano | basement |
| la escalera | stairs |
| el techo | roof |
| la cocina | kitchen |
| el salón | living room |
| la sala de estar | sitting room |
| el comedor | dining room |
| el despacho | study |
| el dormitorio | bedroom |
| la habitación | bedroom |
| el cuarto de baño | bathroom |
| el desván | attic |
| la terraza | balcony/patio |
| el jardín | garden |
| la silla | chair |
| la lámpara | lamp |
| la butaca | armchair |
| la alfombra | rug / carpet |
| los cuadros | pictures |
| la mesa | table |
| la pared | wall |
| el grifo | tap |
| el jabón | soap |
| la toalla | towel |
| el champú | shampoo |
| la ducha | shower |
| el baño | bath |
| el lavavajillas | dishwasher |
| el frigorífico / el frigo | fridge |
| la nevera | fridge |
| la lavadora | washing machine |
| la aspiradora | hoover |
| el plato | plate |
| el tenedor | fork |
| la taza | cup |
| el vaso | glass |
| la cuchara | spoon |
| el cuchillo | knife |
| la sartén | pan |
| el horno | oven |
| la plancha | iron |
| la manta | blanket |
| las sábanas | sheets |
| la almohada | pillow |

| | |
|---|---|
| la cama | bed |
| el estante | shelf |
| el armario | wardrobe |
| la mesilla de noche | bedside table |
| las cortinas | curtains |

**La ropa – Clothes**

| | |
|---|---|
| el traje | suit |
| el abrigo | coat |
| la chaqueta | jacket |
| el impermeable | raincoat |
| el pantalón | trousers |
| la camisa | shirt |
| la blusa | blouse |
| el jersey | jumper |
| la camiseta | t-shirt |
| la chaqueta | cardigan |
| los zapatos | shoes |
| las botas | boots |
| las sandalias | sandals |
| las chanclas | flip-flops |
| las zapatillas de deporte | runners |
| el chándal | tracksuit |
| el vestido | dress |
| el pijama | pyjamas |
| la corbata | tie |
| la bufanda | scarf |
| el sombrero | hat |
| la gorra | cap |
| el cinturón | belt |
| los guantes | gloves |
| los calcetines | socks |
| el bañador | swimsuit |
| el pantalón corto | shorts |
| los vaqueros | jeans |
| la falda | skirt |
| el reloj | watch |
| el collar | necklace |
| la pulsera | bracelet |
| el anillo | ring |
| los pendientes | earrings |
| las joyas | jewellery |

**La comida – Food**

| | |
|---|---|
| la carne | meat |
| la carne de vaca | beef |
| el cerdo | pork |
| el cordero | lamb |
| la ternera | veal |
| el bistec | steak |
| el jamón de york | ham |
| el jamón serrano | cured ham |
| el pollo | chicken |
| el pato | duck |
| el pavo | turkey |
| la chuleta | chop |
| el filete | fillet |
| el pan | bread |
| el pastel | cake |
| el arroz | rice |
| el huevo | egg |
| el azúcar | sugar |
| la mantequilla | butter |
| el aceite | oil |
| el vinagre | vinegar |
| las bebidas | drinks |
| los refrescos | soft drinks |
| el agua con gas | fizzy water |
| el agua sin gas | still water |
| la leche | milk |
| el café | coffee |
| el té | tea |
| el zumo | juice |
| la limonada | lemonade |
| el vino tinto | red wine |
| el vino blanco | white wine |
| garbanzos | chickpeas |
| la cerveza | beer |
| la sidra | cider |
| el pescado | fish |
| los mariscos | shellfish |
| el salmón | salmon |
| la trucha | trout |
| las gambas | prawns |
| los calamares | squid |
| el bacalao | cod |
| la merluza | hake |
| el atún | tuna |
| los mejillones | mussels |
| la sandía | watermelon |
| la manzana | apple |
| la naranja | orange |
| el melocotón | peach |
| la cereza | cherry |
| la piña | pineapple |
| las uvas | grapes |
| el pomelo | grapefruit |
| el plátano | banana |
| la frambuesa | raspberry |
| el albaricoque | apricot |
| la pera | pear |
| el limón | lemon |
| las verduras | vegetables |
| las patatas | potatoes |
| los guisantes | peas |
| los pimientos | peppers |
| los champiñones | mushrooms |
| las judías | beans |
| las zanahorias | carrotts |
| los pepinos | cucumbers |
| las cebollas | onions |
| la lechuga | lettuce |
| la coliflor | cauliflower |
| la col | cabbage |
| las lentejas | lentils |

**Los animales – Animals**

| | |
|---|---|
| la mascota | pet |
| el gato | cat |
| el perro | dog |
| el pez | fish |
| el caballo | horse |
| el conejo | rabbit |
| el pájaro | bird |
| el ratón | mouse |
| la tortuga | tortoise |
| la vaca | cow |
| el cachorro | puppy |
| la rata | rat |
| la oveja | sheep |
| la cabra | goat |
| el lobo | wolf |
| la araña | spider |
| la abeja | bee |
| la cobaya | guinea pig |
| el burro | donkey |
| el cordero | lamb |
| el cerdo | pig |
| el toro | bull |
| el pato | duck |
| el pollo | chicken |
| la rana | frog |
| el gusano | worm |
| la mariposa | butterfly |
| la serpiente | snake |
| el mono | monkey |
| la jirafa | giraffe |
| el oso | bear |
| el delfín | dolphin |
| la cebra | zebra |
| la foca | seal |
| el tiburón | shark |
| el rinoceronte | rhino |
| el león | lion |

**El transporte – Transport**

| | |
|---|---|
| el autobús | bus |
| el avión | plane |
| el barco | boat |
| el camión | truck |
| la camioneta | van |
| la moto | motorbike |
| el tren | train |
| la bicicleta | bicycle |
| el coche | car |
| el billete de ida | one way ticket |
| el billete de ida y vuelta | return ticket |
| el puerto | port |
| la estación de trenes | train station |
| la salida | exit / departures |
| la carretera | road |
| la autopista | motorway |
| la rotonda | roundabout |
| el carril de autobuses | bus lane |
| el paso de peatones | pedestrian crossing |
| el semáforo | traffic lights |
| el puente | bridge |
| el carril de bicicletas | bicycle lane |
| conducir | to drive |
| gasolina | petrol |
| el carné de conducir | drivers licence |
| el cinturón de seguridad | seatbelt |
| el pinchazo | puncture |
| los frenos | brakes |
| el casco | helmet |
| las ruedas | wheels |
| chocar | to crash |

**Las vacaciones – Holidays**

| | |
|---|---|
| el camping | a campsite |
| la tienda | tent |
| el árbol | tree |
| el bosque | woods |
| el campo | countryside |
| la flor | flower |
| la montaña | mountain |
| el río | river |
| el paisaje | landscape |
| el mar | sea |
| la playa | beach |
| la arena | sand |
| el albergue juvenil | youth hostel |
| la montaña rusa | roller-coaster |
| el alojamiento | accommodation |
| alquilar | to rent/hire |
| la vela | sailing |
| el buceo | diving (scuba) |
| tomar el sol | to sunbathe |
| el bronceador | suncream |
| el equipaje | luggage |

**Los países – Countries**

| | |
|---|---|
| Irlanda | Ireland |
| Inglaterra | England |
| Gales | Wales |
| Escocia | Scotland |
| España | Spain |
| Francia | France |
| Alemania | Germany |
| Bélgica | Belgium |
| Países Bajos | Netherlands |
| Dinamarca | Denmark |
| Finlandia | Finland |
| República Checa | Czech Republic |
| Eslovaquia | Slovakia |
| Eslovenia | Slovenia |
| Hungría | Hungry |
| Rumanía | Romania |
| Croacia | Croatia |
| Chipre | Cyprus |
| Estonia | Estonia |
| Letonia | Latvia |
| Lituania | Lithuania |
| Polonia | Poland |

| | |
|---|---|
| Suiza | Switzerland |
| Succia | Sweden |
| Noruega | Norway |
| Nueva Zelanda | New Zealand |
| Los Estados Unidos | USA |
| Grecia | Greece |

**En la ciudad – In the city**

| | |
|---|---|
| el supermercado | supermarket |
| la joyería | jewellery shop |
| la panadería | bakery |
| la zapatería | shoe shop |
| la carnicería | butcher's |
| la floristería | florists |
| la tienda de ropa | clothes shop |
| la peluquería | hairdressers |
| la papelería | stationery shop |
| la tienda | shop |
| ¿dónde está…? | where is…? |
| ¿por dónde se va a…? | how do i get to …? |
| ¿…está lejos? | is… far? |
| todo recto | straight on |
| hasta… | as far as… |
| a la derecha | on the right |
| a la izquierda | on the left |
| cruce el puente | cross the bridge |
| doble la esquina | turn the corner |
| gire a la izquierda | turn left |
| gire a la derecha | turn right |
| la calle | the street |
| la fábrica | factory |
| la plaza de toros | bull ring |
| el castillo | castle |
| el aeropuerto | airport |
| el estadio | stadium |
| el ayuntamiento | town hall |
| la plaza | square |
| la comisaría | police station |
| el aparcamiento | car park |
| la oficina de correos | post office |
| el banco | bank |
| el polideportivo | sports centre |
| el cine | cinema |
| el teatro | theatre |
| el parque | park |
| la piscina | swimming pool |
| la oficina de turismo | tourist office |
| la parada de autobuses | bus stop |
| los grandes almacenes | deparment stores |
| la iglesia | church |
| el museo | museum |
| el parque de atracciones | theme park |

**El colegio – School**

| | |
|---|---|
| la escuela | primary school |
| el instituto | secondary school |
| la clase | class |
| el aula | classroom |
| las estanterías | shelves |
| la ventana | windows |
| el ordenador | computer |
| la puerta | door |
| la basura | bin |
| la pizarra | board |
| el cuaderno | copy |
| el libro | book |
| la carpeta | folder |
| la calculadora | calculator |
| las tijeras | scissors |
| el lápiz | pencil |
| la goma | rubber |
| la regla | ruler |
| el bolígrafo | pen |
| el sacapuntas | pencil sharpener |
| la mochila | school bag |
| irlandés | Irish |
| inglés | English |
| francés | French |
| español | Spanish |
| alemán | German |
| las matemáticas | Maths |
| las ciencias | Science |
| la biología | Biology |
| la química | Chemistry |
| la educación física | PE |
| negocios | Business Studies |
| el hogar | Home EC |
| la religión | Religion |
| el dibujo | Art |
| la historia | History |
| la geografía | Geography |
| sacar buenas notas | to get good grades |
| aprobar | to pass |
| suspender | to fail |
| la música | Music |
| el estuche | pencil case |
| el reloj | clock |
| la informática | Computer studies |
| la física | Physics |
| la carpintería | Wood work |
| los estudios clásicos | Classical studies |

**Los pasatiempos – Hobbies**

| | |
|---|---|
| los deportes | sports |
| jugar al baloncesto | to play basketball |
| jugar al fútbol | to play football |
| jugar al voleibol | to play volleyball |
| jugar a las cartas | to play cards |
| jugar al ajedrez | to play chess |
| hacer natación | to go swimming |
| hacer pesas | to do weights |
| hacer ciclismo | to go cycling |
| hacer gimnasia | to do gymnastics |
| hacer atletismo | to do athletics |
| hacer esquí | to go skiing |
| hacer equitación | to do horseriding |
| el partido | a match |

| | |
|---|---|
| ir al polideportivo | to go to the sports centre |
| ir a la piscina | to go to the pool |
| ir a la bolera | to go bowling |
| la lectura | reading |
| tocar la guitarra | to play the guitar |
| tocar la batería | to play the drums |
| tocar el clarinete | to play the clarinet |
| leer libros | to read books |
| leer tebeos | to read comics |
| leer revistas | to read magazines |
| escuchar música | to listen to music |
| las fiestas | parties |
| ver películas | to watch films |
| ir al cine | to go to the cinema |
| ir al teatro | to go to the theatre |
| ir de compras | to go shopping |
| salir con amigos | to go out with friends |
| charlar | to chat |
| los dibujos animados | cartoons |
| las telenovelas | soaps |
| las películas de terror | horror films |
| las películas de ciencia-ficción | science fiction films |
| las películas de acción | action films |
| las comedias | comedies |
| las redes sociales | social media |
| sacar fotos | to take photos |
| pasear al perro | to walk the dog |
| chatear en línea | to chat online |

**El tiempo – The weather**

| | |
|---|---|
| ¿qué tiempo hace? | what's the weather like? |
| hace buen tiempo | the weather is fine |
| hace mal tiempo | the weather is bad |
| hace calor | it is warm / hot |
| hace frío | it is cold |
| hace sol | it is sunny |
| hace viento | it is windy |
| hace fresco | it is cool |
| hay tormenta | it is stormy |
| hay niebla | it is foggy |
| está nublado | it is cloudy |
| llover (o-ue) | to rain |
| está lloviendo | it is raining |
| llueve | it rains |
| nevar (e-ie) | to snow |
| nieva | it snows |
| está nevando | it is snowing |
| la nube | cloud |
| la lluvia | rain |
| el sol | sun |
| la nieve | snow |
| la escarcha | frost |
| el hielo | ice |
| los chubascos | showers |
| el cielo | the sky |
| la luna | the moon |
| la estrella | the star |
| el pronóstico | the forecast |
| 35 grados | 35 degrees |

**Las tareas domésticas – Household chores**

| | |
|---|---|
| poner la mesa | to set the table |
| arreglar mi dormitorio | to tidy my room |
| hacer la cama | to make my bed |
| quitar la mesa | to clear off the table |
| poner los platos en el lavavajillas | to put the dishes in the dishwasher |
| pasar la aspiradora | to hoover |
| poner la lavadora | to do the laundry |
| cortar el césped | to cut the grass |
| planchar la ropa | to iron my clothes |
| tirar la basura | to put out the bins |
| barrer el suelo | to sweep the floor |
| ayudar en el jardín | to help in the garden |
| cocinar | to cook |
| cambiar las sábanas | to change the sheets |
| fregar los platos | to wash the dishes |
| tender la ropa | to hang out the clothes |
| vaciar el lavaplatos | to empty the dishwasher |
| quitar el polvo | to dust |

**El cuerpo – The body**

| | |
|---|---|
| la cara | face |
| la cabeza | head |
| la garganta | throat |
| el brazo | arm |
| el estómago | stomach |
| el corazón | heart |
| la pierna | leg |
| el pie | foot |
| el tobillo | ankle |
| la rodilla | knee |
| la mano | hand |
| la muñeca | wrist |
| el hombro | shoulder |
| los dedos | fingers |
| la espalda | back |
| el corazón | heart |
| los pulmones | lungs |
| el pelo | hair |
| la oreja | ear |
| el ojo | eye |
| la nariz | nose |
| la boca | mouth |
| los dientes | teeth |
| los labios | lips |
| estar enfermo | to be sick |
| estar resfriado | to have a cold |
| tener la gripe | to have the flu |
| tener tos | to have a cough |
| tener dolor de... | to have a pain in... |
| tener fiebre | to have a temperature |
| estar mareado | to be dizzy |
| toser | to cough |
| la alergia | allergy |
| la receta | prescription |

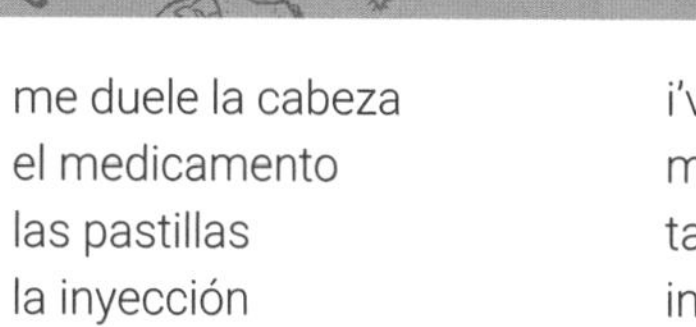

| | |
|---|---|
| me duele la cabeza | i've a headache |
| el medicamento | medicine |
| las pastillas | tablets |
| la inyección | injection |
| el dolor de muelas | toothache |

**Los anuncios – Signs**

| | |
|---|---|
| rebajas | sales |
| agua potable | drinking water |
| abierto todo el año | open all year |
| alquiler de coches | car hire |
| comida para llevar | take away meals |
| calle peatonal | pedestrian street |
| gracias por su visita | thanks for your visit |
| alto riesgo de incendio | high risk of fire |
| no tirar basura | don't litter |
| cerrado por vacaciones | closed for holidays |
| curva peligrosa | dangerous bend |
| pague con tarjeta | pay with credit card |
| prohibido pasar | do not pass |
| no se permite fumar | no smoking |
| no pisar e el césped | do not step on the grass |
| se vende pan | bread for sale |
| entrada | entrance |
| salida | exit |
| facturación | check-in |
| oficina de objetos perdidos | lost property office |
| primeros auxilios | first aid |
| información turística | tourist information |
| andén 3 | platform 3 |
| sala de espera | waiting room |
| ascensor | lift |
| ten cuidado | be careful |
| muebles | furniture |
| electrodomésticos | electrical appliances |
| no tocar | don't touch |
| no sacar fotos | don't take photos |
| firmar aquí | please sign here |
| apagar el móvil | turn off your mobile |

**Expresiones útiles – Useful phrases**

**Greetings and exclamations**

| | |
|---|---|
| ¡Buenos días! | Good Morning |
| ¡Buenas tardes! | Good Afternoon / Good Evening |
| ¡Buenas noches! | Good Night! |
| ¡Feliz cumpleaños | Happy Birthday! |
| ¡Feliz Navidad! | Happy Christmas! |
| ¡Que aproveche! | Enjoy your meal |
| ¡Lo siento! | I'm sorry |
| ¡Bienvenidos! | Welcome! |
| ¡Mucho gusto! | Nice to meet you! |

**Writing a blog**

My best friend

| | |
|---|---|
| Mi mejor amigo se llama Ryan. Lo conozco desde hace tres años. | My best friend's name is Ryan. I've known him for 3 years. |
| Es alto y delgado y tiene el pelo rubio. | He is tall and slim with blonde hair. |
| Es muy simpático y divertido. | He is kind and funny. |
| Vive en la misma calle que yo. | He lives in the same street as me. |

My hobbies

| | |
|---|---|
| En mi tiempo libre me encanta hacer deporte. | In my free time I like to do sports. |
| Juego al fútbol con el equipo de mi colegio. | I play football with my school team. |
| Me gusta la música rock y toco la guitarra. | I like rock music and I play the guitar. |
| Voy al cine todos los fines de semana. | I go to the cinema every weekend. |

My area

| | |
|---|---|
| Vivo en un barrio residencial en las afueras de Limerick. | I live in a residential neighborhood in the suburbs of Limerick. |
| Mi casa está en una calle tranquila cerca de un parque. | My house in a quiet street near a park. |
| En mi barrio hay una panadería, una iglesia y un colegio. | In my neighborhood there is a bakery, a church and a school. |

My daily routine

| | |
|---|---|
| Me levanto a las siete y media de la mañana. | I get up at 7:30am. |
| Desayuno pan tostado con mantequilla y una taza de té. | For breakfast I have toast with butter and a cup of tea. |
| Salgo de casa a las ocho y voy al colegio en autobús. | I leave home at 8:00 and get the bus to school. |
| A la una como un bocadillo en el comedor del colegio. | At 1:00 I have a sandwich in the school canteen. |
| Vuelvo a casa a las tres y media y hago los deberes. | I go home at 3:30 and do my homework. |

My school

| | |
|---|---|
| Voy a un colegio católico de chicas. | I go to a Catholic girl's school. |
| Hay muchas actividades extraescolares y muy buenas instalaciones. | There are lots of extra extracurricular activities and very good facilities. |
| Los profesores son muy estrictos y nos ponen muchos deberes. | The teachers are very strict and give us a lot of homework. |

Holidays: Present tense

| | |
|---|---|
| Estoy aquí en Alicante. | Here I am in Alicante. |
| Hace muy buen tiempo. | The weather is great. |
| Nos alojamos en un piso al lado del mar. | We're staying in an apartment beside the sea. |
| Me encanta la playa y la piscina. | I love the beach and the pool. |

Holidays: Past tense

| | |
|---|---|
| El año pasado hice un intercambio con un chico español. | Last year I did an exchange with a Spanish boy. |
| Lo pasé genial. | I had a great time. |
| Probé muchos platos típicos como la paella. | I tried lots of typical dishes like paella. |

Holidays: Future tense

| | |
|---|---|
| El verano que viene voy a ir a Barcelona. | Next summer I am going to go to Barcelona. |
| Iré en avión con mi familia. | I will go by plane with my family. |
| Vamos a visitar la Sagrada Familia. | We're going to visit the Sagrada Familia. |
| Nos alojaremos en un hotel cerca del centro de la ciudad. | We will stay in a hotel near the city centre. |

**Writing an email**

| | |
|---|---|
| Gracias por tu última carta que recibí ayer. | Thanks for your letter I got yesterday. |
| ¿Qué tal por allí? | How are things there? |
| Siento no haberte escrito antes pero he tenido mucho que hacer. | Sorry for not writing sooner, I had lots to do. |
| Muchas gracias por el regalo que me mandaste. | Thanks for the present you sent me. |
| Muchas gracias por tu amable invitación. | Thanks for your kind invitation. |
| Me encantaría ir a España. | I would love to go to Spain. |
| Cuando vaya a España me gustaría ir a la playa. | When I go to Spain I'd like to go to the beach. |
| Desgraciadamente no puedo visitarte este verano. | Unfortunately I can't visit this summer. |
| Te escribo para invitarte a Irlanda. | I'm writing to invite you to Ireland. |
| Te recogeré en el aeropuerto. | I'll pick you up at the airport. |
| Te escribo para desearte... | I'm writing to wish you... |
| – Feliz cumpleaños. | Happy Birthday. |
| – Feliz Navidad. | Happy Christmas. |
| – Felices Pascuas. | Happy Easter. |
| – Feliz Año Nuevo. | Happy New Year. |
| Da recuerdos a tu familia. | Say hello to your family. |
| Me tengo que ir ahora. | I have to go now. |
| Quedo a la espera de tus noticias. | Looking forward to hearing from you. |

**Exam Checklist**

As you revise each topic, tick it off on the checklist below, it will really help you track your learning and how much you know. Revise small amounts in a regular way from sections 3 and 4 of this exam guide. Going back over topics will really help you to remember them and help keep them fresh in your mind.

| Grammar topic | More revision needed | I know it well |
|---|---|---|
| The simple present tense: regular verbs | | |
| The simple present tense: radical changing verbs | | |
| The simple present tense: reflexive verbs | | |
| The simple present tense: irregular verbs | | |
| The present continuous tense | | |
| The preterite tense | | |
| The imperfect tense | | |
| The present perfect tense | | |
| The 'going to' future tense | | |
| The 'will' future tense | | |
| Adjectives | | |
| Possessive adjectives | | |
| Demonstrative adjectives | | |
| Interrogatives | | |
| The definite article | | |
| The indefinite article | | |
| Important verbs | | |
| Los números – Numbers | | |
| Los días de la semana – The days of the week | | |
| Los meses del año – The months of the year | | |
| Las estaciones – The seasons | | |
| La hora – Time | | |
| La familia – The family | | |
| Los colores – Colours | | |
| Las profesiones – Professions | | |
| La casa – The house | | |
| La ropa – Clothes | | |
| La comida – Food | | |
| Los animales – Animals | | |
| El transporte – Transport | | |
| Las vacaciones – Holidays | | |
| Los países – Countries | | |
| En la ciudad – In the city | | |
| El colegio – School | | |
| Los pasatiempos – Hobbies | | |
| El tiempo – Weather | | |
| Las tareas domésticas – Household chores | | |
| El cuerpo – The body | | |
| Los anuncios – Signs | | |
| Expresiones importantes – Useful phrases | | |

# Map Your Progress!

Tick each paper as you complete it and tick the questions on each paper.

| Junior Cycle Spanish Common Level | Time | SEC 2022 | SEC 2019 sample | Edco Sample A | Edco Sample B | Edco Sample C | Edco Sample D | Edco Sample E | Edco Sample F |
|---|---|---|---|---|---|---|---|---|---|
| **Listening (140 marks)** | | | | | | | | | |
| Question 1 | | | | | | | | | |
| Question 2 | | | | | | | | | |
| Question 3 | | | | | | | | | |
| Question 4 | | | | | | | | | |
| Question 5 | | | | | | | | | |
| Question 6 | | | | | | | | | |
| Question 7 | | | | | | | | | |
| Question 8 | | | | | | | | | |
| **Reading (140 marks)** | | | | | | | | | |
| Question 9 | | | | | | | | | |
| Question 10 | | | | | | | | | |
| Question 11 | | | | | | | | | |
| Question 12 | | | | | | | | | |
| Question 13 | | | | | | | | | |
| Question 14 | | | | | | | | | |
| Question 15 | | | | | | | | | |
| **Writing (80 marks)** | | | | | | | | | |
| Question 16 | | | | | | | | | |
| Question 17 | | | | | | | | | |
| Question 18 | | | | | | | | | |
| **Exam Complete** | | | | | | | | | |

## Remember

- You must answer all sections.
- Pay attention to the marks allocated.
- Plan your time.
- Read instructions carefully.
- Always check back over your answers.

**Study Hub**

**Your free online guide to smarter study.**

**Visit**

**www.edco.ie/onlinestudyhub**

## Junior Cycle Spanish Grading of the Final Examination

| Grade Range | % |
|---|---|
| Distinction | 90 to 100 |
| Higher Merit | 75 but less than 90 |
| Merit | 55 but less than 75 |
| Achieved | 40 but less than 55 |
| Partially Achieved | 20 but less than 40 |
| Not Graded | 0 but less than 20 |

Source: State Examinations Commission, 2022.

## Junior Cycle Learning Outcomes

The specification for Junior Cycle Modern Foreign Languages is organised around three integrated strands.

Strand 1: Communicative Competence

Strand 2: Language Awareness

Strand 3: Socio-cultural Knowledge and Intercultural Awareness

These strands are further broken down into learning outcomes, outlined in the table below. The final examination will assess students' knowledge of **a sample of the outcomes**. The exam is a common level paper set by the State Examinations Commission. The examination will be two hours long and will require students to engage with and respond to stimulus material.

| Strand 1: Communicative Competence | | |
|---|---|---|
| **ELEMENTS** | **Students should be able to:** | |
| **Listening** | 1.1 | identify the general topic of a conversation on familiar topics when it is expressed clearly |
| | 1.2 | recognise frequently-used words and phrases related to areas of immediate relevance and experience, including the language of routine classroom interactions |
| | 1.3 | identify specific information in texts related to familiar topics such as announcements, conversations, simple news items |
| | 1.4 | source, select and share audio stimuli such as songs, conversations, advertisements through appropriate digital technologies |
| **Reading** | 1.5 | recognise the meaning of familiar words and phrases to include everyday signs and notices in public places |
| | 1.6 | understand the general sense of a text on familiar topics |
| | 1.7 | identify specific information in a range of texts dealing with familiar topics |
| | 1.8 | source and use authentic texts to explore topics of relevance through a range of media |
| **Spoken production** | 1.9 | pronounce words accurately enough to be understood, with appropriate intonation |
| | 1.10 | convey simple descriptions, presentations or announcements on familiar topics |
| **Spoken interaction** | 1.11 | interact in routine exchanges with pronunciation and intonation which is clear enough to be understood and with appropriate nonverbal language |
| | 1.12 | use simple polite forms in formal and informal situations such as greetings, thanks, introductions, and respond appropriately |
| | 1.13 | ask and answer questions and exchange ideas, emotions and information on familiar topics in everyday situations |
| | 1.14 | understand and use numbers as appropriate in everyday situations such as shopping, exchanging numbers, sequencing events |
| | 1.15 | take part in routine classroom interactions such as pair and group work, asking questions, language games and activities, asking for help and repetition where necessary |
| | 1.16 | communicate orally with others using digital technologies such as social media |
| **Writing** | 1.17 | write words and create short sentences using various media (emails, letters, blogs, postcards...) on everyday topics with accuracy |
| | 1.18 | write a series of phrases and sentences linked with simple connectors such as but, and, or, as |
| | 1.19 | create texts about aspects of their lives and topics that interest them such as family and friends, school, holidays, leisure activities, fashion, sport, celebrities |
| | 1.20 | write short descriptions of present, past and future events, activities and personal experiences, as well as imaginative texts |
| | 1.21 | fill out forms relevant to their age group and experience |
| | 1.22 | produce and edit texts and interact with others in writing using appropriate digital technologies |

| Strand 2: Language Awareness | | |
|---|---|---|
| **ELEMENTS** | **Students should be able to:** | |
| **Reflecting on how the target language works** | 2.1 | recognise, describe and use language patterns such as word order, verbal system, nouns, adjectives, spelling and punctuation conventions |
| | 2.2 | apply all language learning to creative activities such as producing simple poems, posters, presentations, games and drama |
| | 2.3 | recognise how gender and social conventions influence target language usage |
| **Comparing the target language with other languages they know** | 2.4 | identify similarities and differences between the pronunciation, intonation and rhythm of the target language and that of other languages they know |
| | 2.5 | compare grammar and vocabulary of the target language with that of other languages they know, making connections and distinctions as appropriate |
| **Reflecting on how they learn languages** | 2.6 | identify, share and explain their preferred language-learning strategies |
| | 2.7 | monitor and assess their own learning, using feedback they receive to reflect on what they need to improve and to set goals for improvement |

| Strand 3: Socio-cultural Knowledge and Intercultural Awareness | | |
|---|---|---|
| **ELEMENTS** | **Students should be able to:** | |
| **Learning about relevant facts, people, places and history about the country/ countries related to the target language** | 3.1 | name and describe some features of the target language country/countries such as geographical features, weather, places and landmarks, food |
| | 3.2 | discover and use facts and figures related to the target country/countries such as statistical data, festivals, inventions, famous people |
| | 3.3 | reflect on what they have learned about the country/countries associated with the target language |
| **Learning about traditions, customs and behaviours** | 3.4 | identify and explain some aspects of the target language country/countries in areas such as everyday living, interpersonal relations, customs and behaviours, social conventions |
| | 3.5 | identify and reflect on common stereotypes about the target culture/s, including their own, and explain if and how their attitude towards the target country/countries is evolving |
| | 3.6 | select, process and present information through the appropriate use of digital technologies, and evaluate it for truth and reliability |
| **Comparing their culture with that of the country/ countries related to the target language** | 3.7 | analyse similarities and differences in relation to their peers' lives in the target language country/ countries in areas of daily life such as school, socialising, sport, eating habits |
| | 3.8 | compare and contrast aspects of personal interest in the target language country/countries with those in their own country and present them using a range of media |
| | 3.9 | appreciate how cultural differences influence social relations, such as in greetings and eating together |
| | 3.10 | compare and contrast the use of numbers in the target language country/countries and in their own, with regard to familiar topics such as prices, age, dates, seasons |

2022J012C1EL

2022

Coimisiún na Scrúduithe Stáit
State Examinations Commission

# Junior Cycle Final Examination 2022

# Spanish

## Common Level

## Wednesday 15 June      Afternoon 1:30 - 3:30

360 marks

**Examination Number**

**Day and Month of Birth**

For example, 3rd February is entered as 0302

**Centre Stamp**

| For Examiner Only | |
|---|---|
| 1 | |
| 2 | |
| 3 | |
| 4 | |
| 5 | |
| 6 | |
| 7 | |
| 8 | |
| 9 | |
| 10 | |
| 11 | |
| 12 | |
| 13 | |
| 14 | |
| 15 | |
| 16 | |
| 17 | |
| 18 | |

| For Examiner Only | |
|---|---|
| **Total** | |
| Grade | |

## Instructions

There are **three** sections in this paper.

| | | | |
|---|---|---|---|
| Section A | Listening | 140 marks | 8 questions |
| Section B | Reading | 140 marks | 7 questions |
| Section C | Writing | 80 marks | 3 questions |

Answer **all** questions.

Read the instructions carefully regarding the language to be used when answering the questions.

Write your answers in the spaces provided in this booklet. There is space for extra work at the end of the booklet. Label any such extra work clearly with the question number and part.

Each Listening Comprehension piece will be played **three** times.

This examination booklet will be scanned and your work will be presented to an examiner on screen. Anything that you write outside of the answer areas may not be seen by the examiner.

| Section A | Listening | 140 marks |
|---|---|---|



**Question 1**

Jaime and Raquel are making plans for Friday afternoon. Tick (✓) **one** box only in each question.

**(a)** Jaime y sus amigos van a:

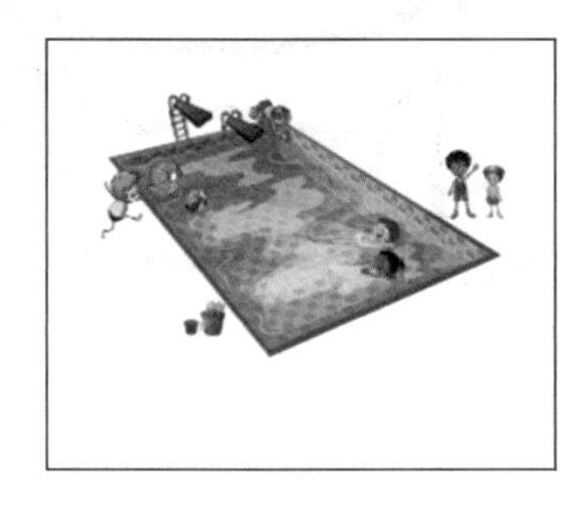

☐ ☐ ☐

**(b)** Jaime y sus amigos van a cenar en un restaurante:

chino ☐

español ☐

italiano ☐

mexicano ☐

**(c)** El restaurante ofrece un descuento de:

12,5% ☐

20% ☐

25% ☐

35% ☐

**(d)** Raquel va a hablar con sus padres:

esta tarde ☐

mañana ☐

**Question 2**

Juan is buying a birthday present for his son Sergio. Tick (✓) **one** box only in each question.

**(a)** ¿Qué día es el cumpleaños de Sergio?

- lunes ☐
- miércoles ☐
- viernes ☐
- domingo ☐

**(b)** ¿Cuántos años cumple Sergio?

- dieciocho ☐
- once ☐
- quince ☐
- ocho ☐

**(c)** ¿Qué recomienda la señora?

- un libro ☐
- una película ☐
- un videojuego ☐
- una revista ☐

**(d)** Juan quiere pagar:

- en efectivo ☐
- con tarjeta de crédito ☐

**Question 3**

Listen carefully to the conversations and fill in the details about each person **in SPANISH**.

**(a)**

| | |
|---|---|
| **Nombre:** | ______ ______ A ______ ______ ______ |
| **Apellidos:** | García Santos |
| **Edad:** | ______________________ años |
| **Cumpleaños:** | el ______________________ de enero |
| **Vive en el centro de:** | ______________________ |
| **Pasatiempo favorito:** | jugar al ______________________ |
| **Hermanos:** | Miguel y Enrique |

**(b)**

| | |
|---|---|
| **Nombre:** | ______ ______ B ______ ______ |
| **Apellidos:** | Sánchez Bermejo |
| **Edad:** | ______________________ años |
| **Cumpleaños:** | el ______________________ de mayo |
| **Vive en las afueras de:** | ______________________ |
| **Pasatiempo favorito:** | escuchar ______________________ |
| **Hermana:** | Julia |

**Question 4**

You will hear a weather forecast for Spain. Answer the questions **in ENGLISH.**

**(a)** When is the weather forecast for?

**(b)** What will the weather be like in the North of Spain?

**(c)** What will the weather be like in Andalusia?



**Question 5**

Conor asks the lady for directions. Answer the questions **in ENGLISH.**

**(a)** How long does the bus journey take?

**(b)** Where is the bus stop?

**(c)** Conor says his teacher is:

Tick (✓) **one** box only.

wonderful ☐

strict ☐

**Question 6**

You will hear an announcement about World Book Day. Answer the questions **in ENGLISH.**

**(a)** When is World Book Day this year?

**(b)** Children can read in public:

Tick (✓) **one** box only.

true ☐

false ☐

**(c)** What special offer is mentioned?



**Question 7**

You will hear a news item about a robbery in a shopping centre. Answer the questions **in ENGLISH.**

**(a)** What shop did the robbery take place in?

**(b)** What time did the thief enter the shop?

**(c)** How did he escape?

**(d)** What are the police doing?

**Question 8**

You will hear an announcement about a ski trip to Candanchú. Answer the questions **in ENGLISH**.

There will be a a pause during the second playing.

**(a)** Who is the ski trip organised for?

| |
|---|

**(b)** What does the price include?

| |
|---|
| |

**(c)** In what year did the ski resort first open?

| |
|---|

**(d)** What colours are mentioned?

| |
|---|
| |
| |
| |

**(e)** Give **three** details about the hotel bedrooms.

| |
|---|
| 1. |
| 2. |
| 3. |

**(f)** Name **three** facilities that the hotel has to offer.

| |
|---|
| 1. |
| 2. |
| 3. |

## Section B Reading 140 marks

**Question 9**

Match the following words and images by filling in the grid.

| | | | |
|---|---|---|---|
| **A** | A la izquierda | **1** | |
| **B** | Escuela | **2** | |
| **C** | Semáforo | **3** |  |
| **D** | Aparcamiento | **4** |  |
| **E** | El puente | **5** |  |
| **F** | A la derecha | **6** |  |
| **G** | Cruce peatonal | **7** |  |
| **H** | Estación de tren | **8** |  |
| **I** | Rotonda | **9** |  |

| Letra | Número |
|---|---|
| A | |
| B | |
| C | |
| D | |
| E | 8 |
| F | |
| G | |
| H | |
| I | |

## Question 10

Look at the images below and match the correct number with the **SPANISH** phrase.

| | NÚMERO |
|---|---|
| Hacer los deberes | |
| Jugar al tenis | |
| Quedar con amigos | |
| Tocar la batería | |
| Usar las redes sociales | |
| Jugar al ajedrez | |

**Question 11**

Read the text and answer the questions **in SPANISH.**

**LA TOMATINA**

**La fiesta del tomate celebra su 75 aniversario este mes de agosto**

| | |
|---|---|
| **Fecha:** | el jueves, 25 de agosto |
| **Lugar:** | Buñol, este de España |
| **Hora:** | empieza a las diez de la mañana |
| **Duración:** | una hora |
| **Ropa**: | se recomienda llevar camiseta y pantalón corto |

**(a)** ¿En qué mes es La Tomatina?

**(b)** ¿Dónde tiene lugar?

**(c)** ¿A qué hora empieza?

**(d)** ¿Qué ropa se recomienda llevar?

## Question 12

Read the text and answer the questions **in SPANISH.**

Me llamo Daniel Stix Soto. Nací en Madrid el veinticuatro de junio de mil novecientos noventa y siete. En mi familia somos cinco, mis padres, mis dos hermanos y yo. Mi madre es española y mi padre es estadounidense. En casa hablamos los dos idiomas: español e inglés.

Soy deportista con discapacidad. Practico el baloncesto en silla de ruedas.

A los catorce años fui el jugador de baloncesto más joven de la historia en participar en una *Champions* en silla de ruedas; es la competición máxima de esta disciplina en Europa. En los Juegos Paralímpicos de Río de 2016 gané una medalla de plata.

Después de pasar un año estudiando en Estados Unidos, volví a Madrid para estudiar Económicas y Relaciones Internacionales, mientras continué mi carrera como jugador de baloncesto profesional.

**(a)** ¿Cuántos hermanos tiene Daniel?

**(b)** ¿De qué nacionalidad es (i) su madre y (ii) su padre?

| (i) su madre: |
|---|
| (ii) su padre: |

**(c)** ¿Qué idiomas hablan en casa?

**(d)** ¿Qué deporte practica Daniel?

**(e)** ¿Qué ganó en 2016?

**(f)** ¿En qué país pasó un año estudiando?

2022

**Question 13**

Read the text messages and answer the questions **in ENGLISH**.

NOTE: Guillermo's messages are in grey and Maria's messages are in green.

●●●●● Movistar 4G 14:50 83%

< **Mensajes** Guillermo

Hola María. ¿Dónde estás? Estoy esperándote enfrente del Ayuntamiento.

Estoy en urgencias en el Hospital Clínico.

¡Ay! ¿Qué te pasó?

Estaba corriendo para coger el autobús y me caí. No podía levantarme. Me duelen los brazos, las piernas y la cabeza.

¡Uf!... Y, ¿cómo llegaste al hospital?

Había una enfermera cerca. Me ayudó y llamó una ambulancia de inmediato.

Y ¿qué te han dicho en el hospital?

Pues, el médico dijo que me he roto la pierna izquierda. ¡Oye! Guillermo, ¿puedes venir al hospital?

Claro que sí. Voy a coger el autobús. Viene uno ahora mismo. Solo tarda ocho minutos.

**(a)** Where is Guillermo waiting for Maria?

**(b)** Where does Maria say she feels pain?

**(c)** Who helped Maria and called the ambulance?

**(d)** What did the doctor say?

**(e)** How is Guillermo going to the hospital?

**(f)** How long will it take him to get there?

## Question 14

Read the text about cycling holidays in Seville and answer the questions **in ENGLISH.**

### Sevilla: Una ciudad para las bicicletas

1. Sevilla es una ciudad ideal para ir en bicicleta porque hace sol durante todo el año. En muy pocos años Sevilla ha cambiado a un modelo de transporte donde la bicicleta es lo más importante.

2. Si vienes a Sevilla vas a disfrutar de ciento setenta kilómetros de carril bici a lo largo de toda la ciudad. Hay un servicio público de alquiler de bicicletas llamado Sevici. Hay un montón de estaciones de Sevici por toda la ciudad que están abiertas las veinticuatro horas del día. ¡Esto es vida!

3. La red de carriles bici llega a todos los barrios de la ciudad. Te puedes mover fácilmente de un sitio a otro de Sevilla, e incluso llegando a algunos lugares en las afueras de la ciudad. La verdad es que Sevilla es un paraíso para los amantes de la bicicleta.

4. Ir en bicicleta por Sevilla es una experiencia única, pero para la seguridad del ciclista se recomienda utilizar casco y chaleco reflectante. Los turistas pueden disfrutar de su clima agradable, la belleza de sus monumentos y claro, sus largos carriles bici. Todo eso se encuentra en muy pocas ciudades del mundo.

5. Para conocer la ciudad se han creado cinco itinerarios temáticos. Puedes visitar el barrio de Triana que es famoso especialmente por la música flamenca y las tiendas de cerámica. Puedes ir en bici desde el Puente de Isabel II con unas bonitas vistas al río Guadalquivir y explorar el quinto río más largo de España.

6. Para tener en cuenta: cuando alquilas una bicicleta de Sevici los treinta primeros minutos de alquiler son gratuitos. Si quieres más información visita nuestra página web: www.sevici.es o llámanos al 900 900 722.

**(a)** Why is Seville an ideal city for cycling? (paragraph 1)

**(b)** How many hours a day are the *Sevici* bicycle stations open? (paragraph 2)

**(c)** The cycle lanes go to all neighbourhoods. (paragraph 3)

Tick (✓) **one** box only:

true ☐

false ☐

**(d)** What can tourists enjoy in Seville? (paragraph 4)

**(e)** What is the Triana neighbourhood famous for? (paragraph 5)

**(f)** What is said about the first thirty minutes of bicycle hire? (paragraph 6)

**(g)** How can you find out more information? (paragraph 6)

## Question 15

Read the text about Mallorca and answer the questions **in ENGLISH.**

**MALLORCA**

Mallorca es la isla más grande y diversa de las Islas Baleares. El aeropuerto de Palma es el tercer aeropuerto más grande de España, está muy cerca de la ciudad de Palma y es muy moderno. Cada año vienen millones de turistas de todas partes de Europa a la isla.

Mallorca es un sitio ideal para las vacaciones con adolescentes porque hay playas bonitas, parques de atracciones y excursiones en barco para divertirse.

Para los que busquen aventura hay actividades como deportes acuáticos, alpinismo y mucho más. Se pueden disfrutar de estas actividades durante todo el año.

Hay que visitar la cosmopolita capital de Mallorca, Palma, que es considerada como una de las joyas del Mediterráneo. El barrio de Santa Catalina es popular porque hay galerías de arte y un mercado donde se puede comprar una gran selección de comida típica.

**(a)** What is said about Palma airport?

**(b)** Why is Mallorca suitable for holidays with teenagers?

**(c)** Name **one** activity recommended for people who seek adventure.

**(d)** Why is the Santa Catalina area popular?

## Section C Writing 80 marks

**Question 16**

Complete the following sentences by inserting the correct **SPANISH** phrase into the space below:

**For example:**

Voy al supermercado para <u>hacer las compras</u>.

| | |
|---|---|
| **todos mis profesores** | **ir al dentista** |
| **te gustaría ir a la discoteca** | **un billete de ida y vuelta** |
| **al sur de España con mi familia** | |

**(a)** Voy de vacaciones ______________________________.

**(b)** Me llevo muy bien con ______________________________.

**(c)** Tengo que ______________________ porque me duele un diente.

**(d)** Quiero comprar ______________________ para el tren.

**(e)** ¡Ana! ¿______________________________ mañana?

**Question 17**

You are staying with the Garcia family in Valencia while doing a Spanish language course. Write an email to your friend **in SPANISH,** giving answers to the following:

**(a)** Describe la familia García.

**(b)** ¿Qué hay en Valencia?

**(c)** ¿Cómo es la comida española?

**(d)** ¿Cómo es el curso de español?

**(e)** ¿Qué haces después de las clases?

**Question 18**

Your exchange student Paco has written to you. Write a response to him **in SPANISH,** giving answers to the following:

Describe tu casa.

Describe tu colegio.

¿Cómo es tu barrio?

¿Cuál es tu rutina diaria?

¿Cuáles son tus pasatiempos?

¿Qué tiempo hace en Irlanda?

¿Qué planes tienes para las vacaciones de verano?

¿Qué hiciste el fin de semana pasado?

## Acknowlegements

### Images

Images on page 3: clipart-library.com; pngtree.com
Image on page 4: coolclips.com
Images on page 9: clipart-library.com; vectorstock.com; shutterstock.com; istockphoto.com
Images on page 10: freepik.com; clipart-library.com; 123rf.com
Image on page 11: www.latomatina.info; https://www.buñol.es/
Image on page 12: www.kiaenzona.com
Image on page 14: shutterstock.com
Image on page 16: www.spain.info/es

### Texts

Text on page 12: adapted from www.kiaenzona.com; www.diariodesevilla.es
Text on page 14: adapted from www.visitasevilla.es
Text on page 16: adapted from www.vacaciones-espana.es; www.abc-mallorca.es; www.aena.es; www.spain.info

Do not write on this page



Junior Cycle Final Examination – Common Level

# Spanish

Wednesday 15 June
Afternoon 1:30 - 3:30

2020J012C1ES

SEC SAMPLE 2019

Coimisiún na Scrúduithe Stáit
State Examinations Commission

# Junior Cycle Final Examination
# Sample Paper

# Spanish

## Common Level

## Time: 2 hours

360 marks

| Examination number | | | | |
|---|---|---|---|---|
| | | | | |

| Centre stamp |
|---|
| |

## Instructions

There are **three** sections in this paper.

| | | | |
|---|---|---|---|
| Section A | Listening | 140 marks | 8 questions |
| Section B | Reading | 140 marks | 6 questions |
| Section C | Written | 80 marks | 3 questions |

Answer **all** questions.

Read the instructions carefully regarding the language to be used when answering the questions.

Write your answers in the spaces provided in this booklet.

Each Listening Comprehension piece will be played **three** times.

This examination booklet will be scanned and your work will be presented to an examiner on screen. Anything that you write outside of the answer areas may not be seen by the examiner.

| Section A | Listening | 140 marks |
|---|---|---|



**Question 1**

Answer the following questions by putting a tick (✓) in the correct box. Tick **one** box only.

**(a)** ¿Qué tarea hace Juan?

☐

☐

☐

**(b)** Los padres de Ana le pagan:

€10 ☐

€15 ☐

€20 ☐

€25 ☐

**(c)** Juan trabaja los sábados:

verdadero ☐

falso ☐

**(d)** Juan recibe dinero de su:

tía ☐

madre ☐

abuela ☐

hermana ☐

**Question 2**

Jaime is buying school supplies for his daughter. Tick (✓) the correct boxes.

**(a)** Marca **seis** cosas de la lista:

| | | | |
|---|---|---|---|
| | | | |
| | | | |
| | | | |
| | | | |

**(b)** ¿Qué libro de texto quiere comprar? Marca **uno** con un tick (✓)

historia ☐

matemáticas ☐

francés ☐

geografía ☐

**(c)** ¿Por qué equipo es famosa la Escuela San Pedro? Marca **uno** con un tick (✓)

fútbol ☐

baloncesto ☐

vóleibol ☐

hockey ☐

## Question 3

Marta describes her uniform. Answer the questions **in Spanish.**



**(a)** Escribe el color del uniforme:

| Uniforme | Color |
|---|---|
| Jersey | |
| Falda | |
| Camisa | |

**(b)** Los alumnos tienen que llevar zapatos negros:

verdadero ☐

falso ☐

**(c)** ¿Qué llevan los alumnos para deportes?

| 1. |
|---|
| 2. |

**(d)** A Marta no le gusta el uniforme. ¿Por qué?

| 1. |
|---|
| 2. |

**Question 4**

Juan telephones the restaurant. Answer the questions **in English.**

**(a)** When is the reservation for?

| DAY | TIME |
|---|---|
| | |

**(b)** What occasion are they celebrating?

**(c)** Where is the table?



**Question 5**

Pedro is in Spanish class. Answer the questions **in English.**

**(a)** Why was Pedro unable to do his homework?

**(b)** What does the teacher ask him for?

**(c)** Why does Pedro have to study tonight?

**Question 6**

You will hear a supermarket announcement. Answer the questions **in English.**

**(a)** What fruit is on offer today? Tick (✓) **three** of the following:

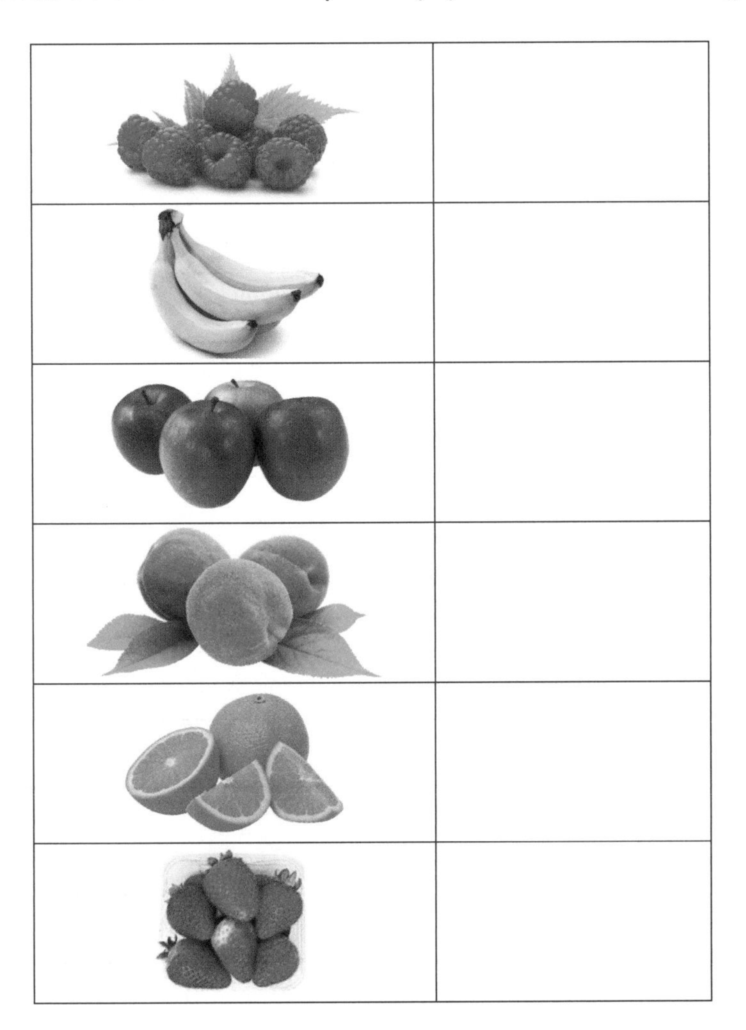

**(b)** Name **three** types of meat that are on offer.

**(c)** How much is a bottle of olive oil?

**(d)** Until when are the offers valid?

**Question 7**

You will hear an advertisement about an apartment for rent. Answer the questions **in English.**

**(a)** Where in Torremolinos is the apartment?

**(b)** What rooms are there in the apartment?

**(c)** Name **three** of the electrical items in the kitchen.

**(d)** What facilities are there in the area?

**Question 8**

School students are going on a tour to Barcelona.

Answer the questions **in English.**

There will be a pause during the second playing.



**(a)** When exactly is the school tour taking place?

| DATE | MONTH |
|---|---|
| | |

**(b)** What will the group do on Monday?

| |
|---|

**(c)** What will the students eat for breakfast?

| |
|---|

**(d)** Name **three** items they should bring to the *Tibidabo* Attraction Park.

| |
|---|
| |
| |

**(e)** What is said about the *Camp Nou*? Give **two** details.

| |
|---|
| |

**(f)** What is *Las Arenas* **and** what can they do there?

| |
|---|
| |

| Section B | Reading | 140 marks |
|---|---|---|

**Question 9**

Match the product with the shop by filling in the grid.

| PRODUCTOS | TIENDAS |
|---|---|
| A Pulseras | 1 PANADERÍA |
| B Pan | 2 LA CARNICERÍA |
| C Sellos | 3 LA FARMACIA |
| D Gambas | 4 PAPELERIA |
| E Antibióticos | 5 La VERDULERÍA |
| F Cuadernos | 6 JOYERÍA |
| G Salchichas | 7 La Pescadería |
| H Zanahorias | 8 CORREOS |

| Letra | Número |
|---|---|
| A | |
| B | |
| C | 8 |
| D | |
| E | |
| F | |
| G | |
| H | |

**Question 10**

Look at the images below and match the correct number with the **Spanish** phrase.

| | NÚMERO |
|---|---|
| Practicar la vela | |
| Reservar una habitación | |
| Montar a caballo | |
| Leer un libro | |
| Ver la televisión | |
| Escuchar la música | |

**Question 11**

John is staying with his Spanish friend Rafa in Alicante. Read the text messages and answer the questions **in English**.

NOTE: Rafa's messages are in grey and John's messages are in green.

●●●●● Movistar 4G 2:34 75%

Mensajes Rafa

¿Qué tal el primer día?

¡Bien! Estoy en la clase de nivel intermedio y el profe es simpático y divertido.

¿Y tus compañeros?

Parecen abiertos. Hay cuatro italianos, tres francesas y dos alemanes.

¿A qué hora vuelves a casa?

A las cinco y cuarto.

¿Quieres venir conmigo al polideportivo entonces?

Sí, sí. ¿Puedo invitar a mi clase?

Claro ¡Espero que jueguen al fútbol mejor que tú!

Mensaje de texto

1. Describe the teacher.

2. Where are John's classmates from?

3. At what time is John returning home?

4. Where does Rafa suggest they go?

5. What question does John ask Rafa?

**Question 12**

Read the text and answer the questions **in English.**

¡Hola! Me llamo Lele Pons. Soy actriz, cantante, presentadora, modelo y estrella de *YouTube*. Nací en Venezuela el veinticinco de junio de mil novecientos noventa y seis. Cuando tenía cinco años, mi familia y yo nos fuimos a vivir a Estados Unidos.

Soy alta y delgada con los ojos marrones y el pelo rubio. Soy abierta, trabajadora y muy habladora. Mi lengua materna es el español, pero también hablo inglés e italiano.

A los quince años empecé a crear vídeos cortos en línea. Los vídeos eran muy populares y ahora tengo más de veintidós millones de seguidores en Internet. Se dice que soy la bloguera de habla española más influyente en las redes sociales en todo el mundo.

**(a)** When was Lele born?

| DATE | MONTH | YEAR |
|---|---|---|
| | | |

**(b)** How does she describe her personality?

**(c)** What **three** languages does she speak?

**(d)** What did Lele do when she was 15?

**(e)** How do we know Lele is popular on the Internet? Give **full** details.

**Question 13**

Read the text and answer the questions **in English.**

## Parque Europa en Madrid.

**1.** El Parque Europa se encuentra a unos veintiséis kilómetros de Madrid. Tiene réplicas de unos dieciocho monumentos famosos de Europa. Entre ellos se puede ver la Torre Eiffel, el Puente de Londres y mucho más. Es muy agradable dar un paseo por este parque y disfrutar de las actividades que ofrece para toda la familia. Sobre todo se recomienda visitarlo en el mes de septiembre cuando hace menos calor.

**2.** El parque está abierto al público todos los días de la semana de nueve de la mañana a diez de la noche. La entrada al parque es completamente gratuita. Es un espacio verde, ya que cuenta con unos cinco mil árboles y tres lagos. Desde Madrid se puede llegar en autobús, en metro o en tren. Si viajas en coche hay un aparcamiento que cuesta tres euros al día.

**3.** En el parque hay dos restaurantes que están abiertos durante todo el año. El restaurante Mirador de Europa tiene una amplia terraza cubierta, con grandes vistas al parque. Este restaurante se especializa en comida típica española como la paella. Aquí se pueden hacer celebraciones privadas como comidas de grupo o cumpleaños. El menú infantil cuesta seis euros, incluye bebida y postre.

**4.** Entre las atracciones está la zona infantil con capacidad para más de cien niños. Allí hay mini coches de Fórmula 1, un campo de mini-golf, un circuito de coches safari y un tren eléctrico. Además, hay una granja con una gran variedad de animales exóticos como tortugas gigantes, tigres, serpientes y canguros.

**(a)** Where is *Parque Europa* situated? (paragraph 1)

| |
|---|
| |

**(b)** What month should you visit the park **and** why? (paragraph 1)

| MONTH | REASON WHY |
|---|---|
| | |

**(c)** What are the opening hours of the park? (paragraph 2)

| |
|---|
| |

**(d)** How can you travel to the park from Madrid? (paragraph 2)

| |
|---|
| |

**(e)** What events can be celebrated in the restaurant? (paragraph 3)

| |
|---|
| |

**(f)** What is said about the children's menu? (paragraph 3)

| |
|---|
| |
| |

**(g)** Name **two** attractions for children. (paragraph 4)

| |
|---|
| |
| |

**(h)** Name **two** exotic animals you can see on the farm. (paragraph 4)

| |
|---|
| |
| |

**Question 14**

Read the text about Mexico City and answer the questions **in English.**

## La ciudad de México.

La ciudad de México es una de las ciudades más grandes del mundo. Tiene una población de unos veinte millones de habitantes. Para disfrutar de unos días en la ciudad se recomienda visitar los lugares más populares como:

**La Plaza de la Constitución:** la Plaza Mayor está en el centro histórico. Es un espacio público para pasar una tarde muy agradable. Hay actos culturales como conciertos, exposiciones y ferias de libros.

**El Acuario Inbursa:** se abrió en el año 2014. Visitar el acuario es una experiencia única. Es una gran atracción turística porque contiene más de catorce mil ejemplares de especies, entre ellos los conocidos pingüinos de la Antártida.

**El Museo de Bellas Artes:** es el edificio más bonito de la ciudad. Además de exposiciones de obras de arte, se puede asistir a un espectáculo de ópera o de ballet. Para entrar en el museo hay descuentos para los alumnos si presentan la tarjeta de estudiante.

El autobús turístico es el método de transporte más rápido para ver la ciudad. Es muy fácil subirse y bajarse en los sitios más importantes. El autobús pasa cada cuarto de hora.

**(a)** What is said about the population of Mexico City?

**(b)** Name the cultural events that take place in the *Plaza de la Constitución*.

**(c)** Why is the *Inbursa* Aquarium popular with tourists?

**(d)** How can students get a discount for the Art Museum?

**(e)** What is said about the tourist bus?

| Section C | Writing | 80 marks |
|---|---|---|

SEC SAMPLE 2019

**Question 15**

Complete the following sentences by inserting the correct **Spanish** phrase into the space below:

**For example:**

Voy al parque con mis amigos para ___*jugar al fútbol*______.

| | |
|---|---|
| **dormir hasta las doce de la mañana** | **hacer exámenes** |
| **charlar con mis primos** | **tomar una aspirina** |
| **ponerme una chaqueta y una bufanda** | **ir a la playa** |

**(a)** Me encanta ____________________________________________en el móvil.

**(b)** Si hace sol mañana voy a ________________________________________.

**(c)** En el colegio no me gusta nada ____________________________________.

**(d)** Cuando me duele la cabeza tengo que _______________________________.

**(e)** Si hace frío suelo ______________________________________________.

**(f)** Cuando tengo sueño quiero _______________________________________.

## Question 16

You are staying in a hotel in Granada with your family. Write a blog **in Spanish,** giving answers to the following:

**(a)** ¿Dónde está el hotel?

**(b)** ¿Qué te gusta más de Granada?

**(c)** ¿Probaste la comida española?

**(d)** ¿Qué tiempo hace en Granada?

**(e)** ¿Qué haces todos los días?

**Mi Blog**

**Question 17**

Your Spanish exchange student Pilar has emailed you with some information about herself and her life in Spain. Write a response **in Spanish** to her questions below:

Hola, me llamo Pilar y soy de Salamanca. No somos muchos en mi familia. Vivo con mi madre y con mi hermano Pablo en un piso en el centro.

¿Cómo es tu familia?

Salamanca es una ciudad animada. Hay una universidad muy famosa y vienen muchos turistas, especialmente en verano. En mi barrio hay muchas tiendas, supermercados y casas antiguas.

¿Qué hay en tu barrio?

Mi colegio es muy grande. Hay novecientos alumnos y setenta profesores. Es mixto y hay unas instalaciones muy buenas.

Describe tu colegio.

Este fin de semana voy a ir al cine con mis amigos. Me encantan las comedias.

¿Qué planes tienes tú para el fin de semana?

| |
|---|
| |
| |
| |
| |

Mi mejor amiga se llama Paula. Es muy simpática y divertida.

¿Cómo es tu mejor amigo/amiga?

| |
|---|
| |
| |
| |
| |

Pues yo me levanto a las siete y media de la mañana y voy al colegio en autobús con mis amigos.

Describe tu rutina diaria.

| |
|---|
| |
| |
| |
| |

El verano pasado fui a visitar a mi prima Julia que vive en el sur de España. ¡ Me lo pasé bomba!

¿Y qué hiciste tú el verano pasado?

| |
|---|
| |
| |
| |
| |

SEC SAMPLE 2019

**Acknowledgements**

**Images**

Images on page 27 : tenor.com; devotedtodog.com; patriciahaueiss.com

Images on page 28: sccpre.cat; goodfreephotos.com; all-free-download.com; clipart-library.com; learnenglishkids.britishcouncil.org

Images on page 31: finefruitsdirect.co.uk; picserver.org; pngimg.com; wikimedia.org; harrisfarm.com.au

Image on page 33: thesefootballtimes.com

Images on page 34: vidaltiendas.com; pixabay.com/es; guiadoshermanas.com; paginas.seccionamarilla.com; iitadvisors.com; diysolarpanelsv.com; destinationcadiz.com; www.cityplan.es

Images on page 35: holzlebn.at; mlandindia.com; yawarra.com.au; calgaryreads.com; theteachersdigest.com; jing.fm

Image on page 37: www.celebvogue.com

Images on page 38: erasmusu.com; susanaclavero.wordpress.com

Image on page 40: pixabay.com

**Texts**

Text on page 38: parqueeuropa.es



Junior Cycle Final Examination – Common Level

# Spanish

Sample Paper

Time: 2 hours

SAMPLE A

# Junior Cycle Final Examination
## Sample Paper A

# Spanish

## Common Level

Time: 2 hours

360 marks

| Examination number | | | | |
|---|---|---|---|---|
| | | | | |

## Instructions

There are **three** sections in this paper.

| | | | |
|---|---|---|---|
| Section A | Listening | 140 marks | 8 questions |
| Section B | Reading | 140 marks | 7 questions |
| Section C | Writing | 80 marks | 3 questions |

Answer **all** questions.

Read the instructions carefully regarding the language to be used when answering the questions.

Write your answers in the spaces provided in this booklet.

| Section A | Listening | 140 marks |
|---|---|---|



**Question 1**

Answer the following questions by putting a tick (✓) in the correct box. Tick **one** box only.

**(a)** La fiesta de Lorena es el viernes.

verdadero ☐

falso ☐

**(b)** ¿A qué hora van a quedar para ir a la fiesta?

6:45 ☐

7:00 ☐

7:15 ☐

7:30 ☐

**(c)** ¿Qué va a llevar Jorge a la fiesta?

☐

☐

☐

☐

**(d)** ¿Qué va a llevar Patri a la fiesta?

☐

☐

☐

☐

**Question 2**

Marta is going to the shop to pick up some groceries. Tick (✓) the correct boxes.

**(a)** ¿Cuánto tiempo ha pasado Marta en el autobús?

- 5 minutos ☐
- 15 minutos ☐
- 25 minutos ☐
- 50 minutos ☐

**(b)** ¿Qué va a hacer el padre de Marta para la cena?

- una paella ☐
- una pizza ☐
- una tortilla ☐
- una sopa ☐

**(c)** Marca **cuatro** cosas que va a comprar Marta.

### Question 3

Antonia describes a school trip to Madrid. Answer the questions **in Spanish**.

**(a)** Antonia y sus compañeros fueron a Madrid en autobús.

verdadero ☐

falso ☐

**(b)** Marca **tres** sitios turísticos que visitaron en Madrid.

| | |
|---|---|
| El museo del Prado | |
| El museo Reina Sofía | |
| El parque del Retiro | |
| La Puerta del Sol | |
| El estadio Bernabéu | |
| El Palacio Real | |

**(c)** ¿Qué compraron en los mercadillos? Menciona **dos** cosas.

**(d)** ¿Qué tiempo hizo en Madrid?

yzngfr
Visit www.e-xamit.ie

SAMPLE A

**Question 4**

María calls her friend Pablo. Answer the questions **in English**.

**(a)** Where does María want to go?

**(b)** Why can Pablo not go on Friday?

**(c)** When do they agree to meet?

| DAY | TIME |
|---|---|
| | |



**Question 5**

Marta is in maths class. Answer the questions **in English.**

**(a)** Why was Marta unable to do her homework?

**(b)** Has Marta got a note from her parents?

**(c)** At what time does Marta have to return to clean the classroom?

## Question 6

You will hear a department store announcement. Answer the questions **in English**.

**(a)** What items for the beach are on offer today? Tick (✓) **three** of the following.

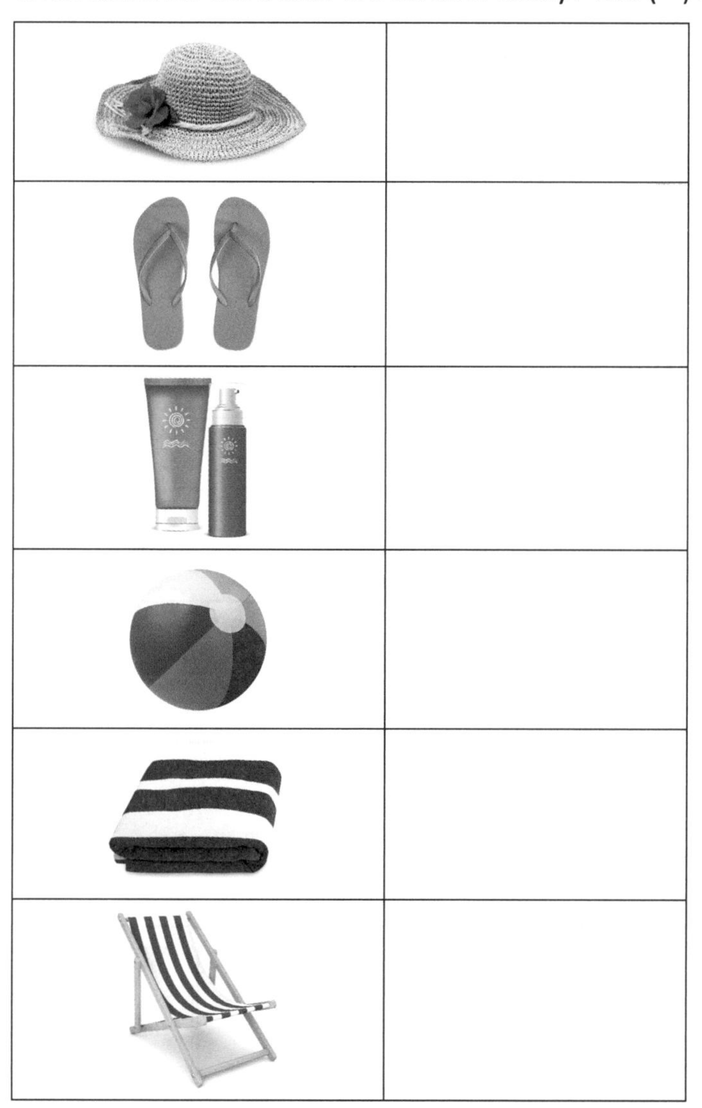

**(b)** What is the percentage discount on the beach items?

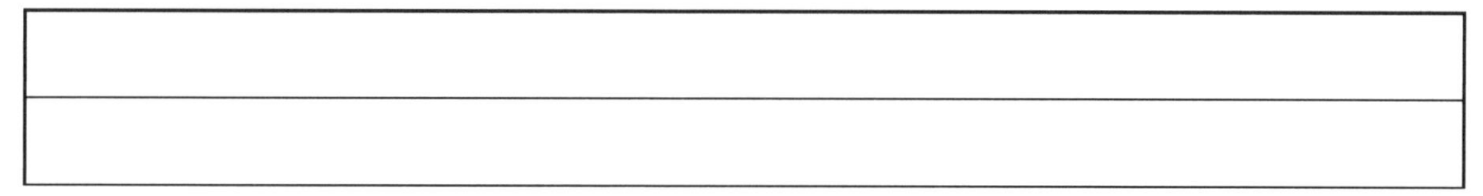

**(c)** Name **two** types of clothing on sale for half price in the fashion department.

**(d)** Until when are the offers valid?

SAMPLE A

**Question 7**

You will hear an advertisement about an apartment for rent. Answer the questions **in English**.

**(a)** Where in Torrevieja is the apartment?

**(b)** Name **four** of the electrical items in the kitchen.

**(c)** What is said about the balcony? Give **two** details.

**(d)** What is the price of renting the apartment for a week?

## Question 8

Laura describes a summer camp she did during the summer. Answer the questions **in English**.

**(a)** How long did Laura spend at the camp?

**(b)** Name **three** sports she did at the camp.

**(c)** What is said about the food at the camp? Give **two** details.

**(d)** How many girls slept in each dormitory?

**(e)** How has she kept in touch with her new friends?

**(f)** When does she hope to see her new friends again?

**Question 9**

Match the sign with the place in which you might find it by filling in the grid.

|  |  |
|---|---|
| **A** Los probadores | **1** El zoo |
| **B** ¡Alerta, tiburón! | **2** El cine |
| **C** Se venden revistas | **3** El aeropuerto |
| **D** ¡Peligro, monos! | **4** La estación de trenes |
| **E** Electrodomésticos | **5** La tienda de ropa |
| **F** Palomitas | **6** Los grandes almacenes |
| **G** Facturación | **7** El quiosco |
| **H** Andén | **8** La playa |

| Letra | Número |
|---|---|
| A | |
| B | |
| C | 7 |
| D | |
| E | |
| F | |
| G | |
| H | |

**Question 10**

Look at the images below and match the correct number with the **Spanish** phrase.

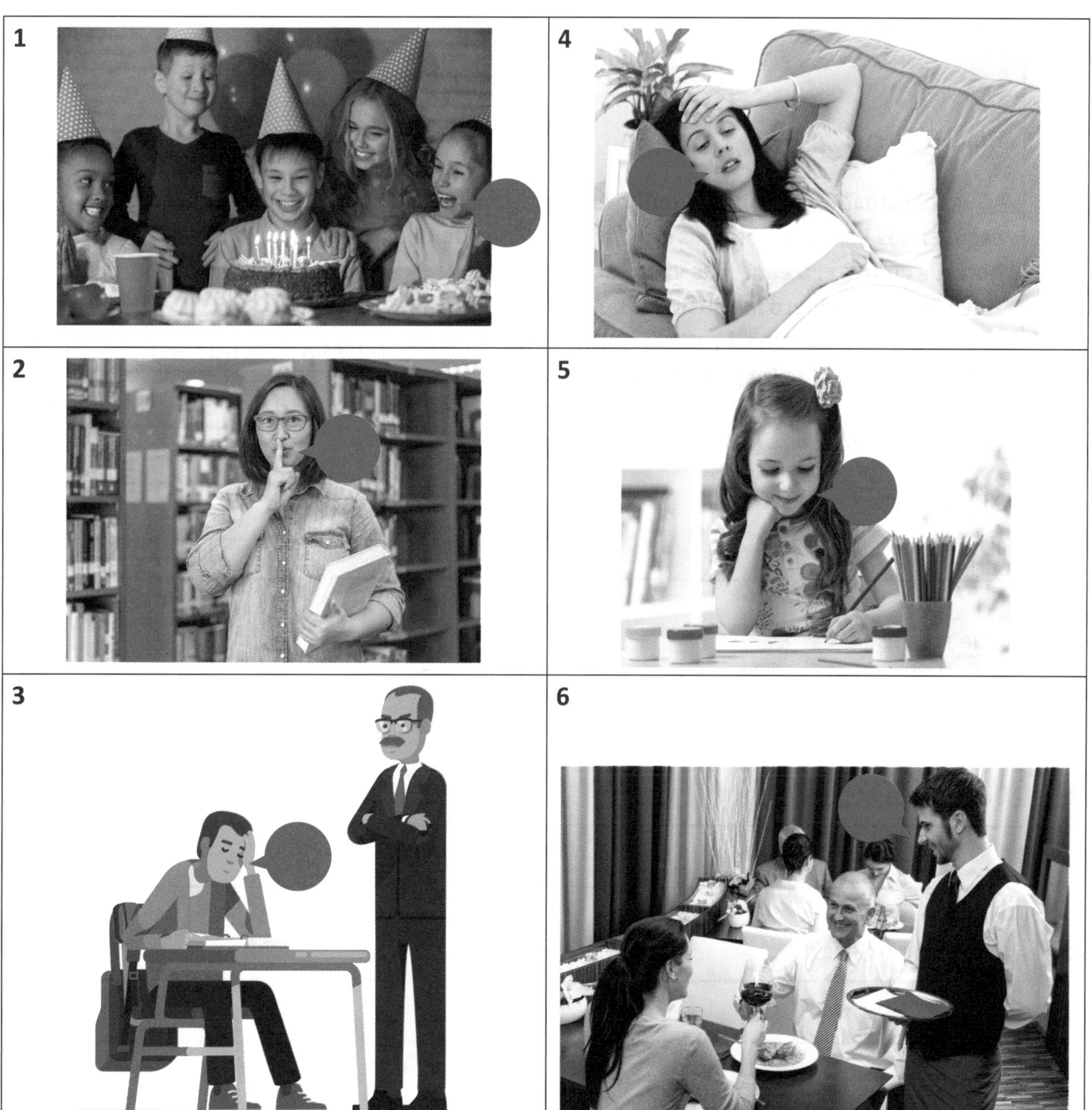


| | Número |
|---|---|
| Profe, no tengo mi cuaderno. | |
| ¡Que aproveche! | |
| ¡Silencio, por favor! | |
| ¡Me encanta dibujar! | |
| ¡Feliz cumpleaños! | |
| No me siento muy bien. | |

ubbrfx
Visit www.e-xamit.ie

SAMPLE A

## Question 11

Read the postcard and answer the questions **in Spanish**.

Andorra, 29 de diciembre

Hola, Gilberto:

¿Qué tal estás? Estoy con mi familia en una estación de esquí en los Pirineos. Estamos alojados en un pequeño hotel de cuatro estrellas. Las vistas son increíbles. Hace mucho frío pero me gusta la nieve. Nos pasamos todo el día esquiando en la montaña. Mañana vamos a patinar. Te veré este fin de semana.

¡Hasta pronto!

Miguel

Gilberto Aguilar Mayans

C/ San Fermín 2º B

Madrid,

España

28001

**(a)** ¿Qué mes es?

**(b)** ¿Dónde está Miguel?

**(c)** ¿Qué tiempo hace?

**(d)** ¿Qué va a hacer Miguel mañana?

## Question 12

Read the text and answer the questions **in Spanish**.

Me llamo José. Soy de Madrid pero vivo en Francia con mis padres. Tenemos una casa nueva en la zona antigua de París. Soy hijo único. En mi tiempo libre me encanta jugar al baloncesto, hacer pesas y nadar. No me gusta mucho leer. Soy alumno en un colegio internacional en París y trabajo a tiempo parcial como camarero. Mi plato favorito es hamburguesa con patatas fritas. No me gustan las naranjas, ni las manzanas ni los plátanos. La semana que viene voy a empezar clases particulares de batería. Tengo muchas ganas de aprenderla y tocar en un grupo algún día porque me encanta la música rock.



**(a)** ¿En qué ciudad vive José?

**(b)** ¿Cuántos hermanos tiene José?

**(c)** ¿Cuáles son sus pasatiempos?

**(d)** ¿Cuál es su trabajo?

**(e)** ¿Cuál es su plato favorito?

**(f)** ¿Qué va a hacer la semana que viene?

**Question 13**

Fito is looking for advice on how to entertain an exchange student who is coming to stay with him. Read the online forum and answer the questions **in English**.

@Fito: Hola chicos, una pregunta: ¿qué actividades me recomendáis para hacer con un intercambio? Mañana viene un chico francés para quedarse en mi casa un mes para practicar español. No sé mucho francés porque he empezado a estudiarlo este año, pero seguro que él habla español muy bien porque es un año mayor que yo. Me gustaría llevarlo a algún sitio chulo o a hacer alguna actividad interesante.

@Carmen: Hola, pues ¿le has preguntado por sus aficiones? Si le gustan los deportes al aire libre, por ejemplo, la escalada o el senderismo, podrías llevarlo al Parque Natural. Estuve el pasado fin de semana, y ahora en primavera está precioso lleno de flores y no hace mucho calor.

@Cristina: Bueno, eso si le gusta el aire libre. A lo mejor prefiere ir a los bolos. Cuando estuve en Irlanda fui a jugar a los bolos y lo pasamos genial. La bolera es un sitio superchulo. ¿Hay alguna por donde vives? Es bueno para conocer gente y puedes llevar también a tus amigos.

@Carlos: ¿Has probado una sala de escape? Te encierras en una habitación con un grupo de gente, tenéis que resolver una prueba y no podéis salir hasta que lo conseguís. El problema es que tiene que hablar bien español para entender las instrucciones.

@Mohammed: Pregúntale si le gustan los deportes. Seguro que le gusta el fútbol. Si al lado de tu casa hay un polideportivo con canchas de baloncesto o campos de fútbol, no tienes por qué preocuparte. Cuando hice mi intercambio en Bordeaux, fui a un campamento de deportes. ¡Hasta fui a nadar porque había piscina!

1. What nationality is the exchange student who is coming to stay with Fito?

2. When did Carmen visit the nature reserve?

3. What activity does Cristina recommend?

4. Why does Carlos think an escape room activity might be difficult?

5. What does Mohammed suggest they should do?

**Question 14**

Read the text and answer the questions **in English**.

## La Tomatina: una fiesta con tomates

**1.** La Tomatina es un festival que se celebra en un pueblo llamado Buñol, en Valencia, que está situado en el este de España, y que tiene como objetivo una guerra de tomates. El último miércoles de agosto todos los ciudadanos y visitantes se reúnen en el centro del pueblo para lanzarse tomates unos a otros durante una hora u hora y media. El origen de la fiesta no es muy claro: algunos dicen que todo empezó porque una persona enfadada con el alcalde del pueblo le tiró unos tomates para mostrar su descontento. Otros dicen que, en realidad, fue una pelea entre amigos que terminó en una lucha de alimentos. Y otra teoría es que fue un camión que derramó los tomates que transportaba. Lo único cierto es que esta fiesta se empezó a celebrar en 1944 y que se ha celebrado desde entonces con excepción de algunos años por el gobierno de Franco. Se celebra sin interrupción desde 1959.

**2.** El día anterior a la fiesta los vecinos cubren las ventanas y las puertas de las casas para protegerlas de los lanzamientos de tomates. El día de la fiesta, los participantes, vestidos con ropa cómoda, se dan cita en las calles del pueblo y esperan con emoción la llegada de camiones llenos de tomates. Después del sonido de un cohete, los camiones llenos hasta arriba avanzan por el pueblo mientras algunas personas subidas en ellos lanzan tomates a la gente reunida en sus calles.

**3.** Para la fiesta se usan unas ciento veinte toneladas de tomates que dejarán a las personas manchadas de rojo y pulpa. Después del sonido del cohete que anuncia el final de la guerra de tomates, las personas se pueden limpiar los restos en duchas que el ayuntamiento pone al servicio de los participantes.

**4.** Si quieres participar debes saber que hay un límite de participantes, no se permiten más de dos mil personas, y que la mayoría de visitantes extranjeros a esta fiesta son australianos, japoneses, británicos y estadounidenses.

**(a)** When and where exactly is La Tomatina celebrated? (paragraph 1)

| WHEN | WHERE |
|---|---|
| | |

**(b)** How long does the tomato fight last? (paragraph 1)

**(c)** What do the residents do the day before the festival, and why? (paragraph 2)

| WHAT | REASON WHY |
|---|---|
| | |

**(d)** What quantity of tomatoes is used in the festival? (paragraph 3)

**(e)** What service does the town council provide to participants? (paragraph 3)

**(f)** What is the maximum number of people that can take part? (paragraph 4)

**(g)** Where do most of the foreign participants come from? Give **full** details. (paragraph 4)

**Question 15**

Read the text about a festival in Bolivia and answer the questions **in English**.

## Carnavales de Chapaco, Bolivia

**1.** Bolivia está dividida en distintos departamentos. Uno de ellos se llama Tarija, situado en el sur del país, y es conocido por su carnaval, un carnaval especial porque celebra el valor de la amistad, y todas las familias salen a bailar vestidas de alegres colores. El Carnaval se llama Chapaco de Tarija y tiene lugar durante todos los días que dura la festividad. Unos días antes del comienzo unos hombres a caballo anuncian la festividad tocando un tambor.

**2.** La fiesta comienza el jueves antes del comienzo del carnaval con la Fiesta de los Compadres donde los hombres se regalan cestas que contienen quesos, fruta, caramelos, tortas, globos y serpentinas. Estos regalos son símbolos de amistad. Cuando los hombres se encuentran en la plaza se dan un abrazo como pacto de amistad y se intercambian las cestas.

**3.** El mismo día, a la semana siguiente, lo mismo ocurre con las mujeres. Por la mañana, el pueblo se llena de mujeres solas que, al igual que los hombres, se regalan canastas de frutas. A mediodía, todas las familias comen al aire libre en la plaza comida tradicional como chancho a la cruz, que es cerdo hecho a la barbacoa, o el picante de pollo, y se bebe chicha con o sin alcohol. Por la tarde, todo el mundo baila al ritmo de sonidos tradicionales y aparecen entre el público las comparsas, grupos de personas que cantan canciones reivindicativas sobre políticos y personas famosas para quejarse o reírse de situaciones que tuvieron lugar durante el año.

**4.** Hay días especiales durante todo el período de carnaval. Por ejemplo, el viernes es el día de la Reina del Carnaval donde se elige a la representante del carnaval ese año; el domingo es el Corso Infantil para los más pequeños y también el Día de la Albahaca, que consiste en dar ofrendas a la Madre Tierra. El Carnaval termina el Domingo de Tentación cuando se encierra al diablo en una danza donde la gente usa disfraces con cuernos.

**(a)** Where is Tarija situated? (paragraph 1)

**(b)** Who announces the start of the festival? (paragraph 1)

**(c)** Name **three** things that the men carry in baskets during the *Fiesta de los Compadres*. (paragraph 2)

**(d)** What happens at midday on the day the women celebrate? (paragraph 3)

**(e)** What exactly is *chancho a la cruz*? (paragraph 3)

**(f)** Who do the *comparsas* (singing groups) sing songs about? (paragraph 3)

**(g)** What happens on the Friday of the festival? (paragraph 4)

## Section C Writing 80 marks

**Question 16**

Complete the following sentences by inserting the correct **Spanish** phrase into the space below:

**For example:**

Fui a España de vacaciones ***el verano pasado*** .

| | |
|---|---|
| **suelo llevar** | **de la mañana** |
| **al final de la calle** | **voy a visitar** |
| **mandar correos electrónicos** | **para venir al instituto** |

**(a)** Uso internet para ______________________________.

**(b)** Me levanto a las siete ______________________________.

**(c)** El cine está ______________________________.

**(d)** Cuando está lloviendo ______________________ un impermeable.

**(e)** Este fin de semana ______________________ a mi tía.

**(f)** Cojo el metro ______________________________.



SAMPLE A

**Question 17**

You are staying with a Spanish family in Madrid. Write a blog **in Spanish**, giving answers to the following:

**(a)** ¿Dónde vive la familia exactamente?

**(b)** ¿Qué te gusta más de Madrid?

**(c)** ¿Visitaste muchos sitios interesantes?

**(d)** ¿Tienes un nuevo amigo en Madrid?

**(e)** ¿Qué vas a hacer el fin de semana que viene?

**Mi Blog**

**Question 18**

Your Spanish friend Raúl has emailed you with some information about himself and his school in Spain. Write a response **in Spanish** to his questions below:

¡Hola! ¿Qué tal? Gracias por el correo electrónico. Es un colegio mixto y está en el centro de la ciudad. Hay muy buen ambiente en mi colegio. Hay una biblioteca, dos laboratorios y una sala de informática.

¿Cómo es tu colegio?

No tengo que llevar uniforme en mi colegio. Normalmente cuando hace calor llevo una camiseta con mangas cortas y unos pantalones cortos y cuando hace frío suelo llevar un abrigo, un jersey y unos vaqueros.

¿Qué ropa llevas al colegio normalmente?

Los profesores en mi colegio son bastante estrictos y hay muchas normas aquí. Se prohíbe fumar por supuesto y no se debe correr en los pasillos.

¿Hay muchas normas en tu colegio?

Mi día escolar termina a las cinco menos cuarto y cojo el autobús a mi casa. Normalmente hago mis deberes y miro la televisión. Ceno con mi familia a las nueve.

¿Qué haces después del colegio normalmente?

Estudio muchas asignaturas en mi colegio, por ejemplo la lengua castellana y literatura, la geografía, las matemáticas y la música. Mi asignatura favorita es la música porque me interesa mucho cantar y escuchar música. Toco la trompeta y el violín.

¿Qué te gusta hacer en tu tiempo libre?

El fin de semana pasado fui al concierto de Ed Sheeran con mi amiga Marta. Pasamos toda la noche bailando y cantando. Antes del concierto fuimos a un restaurante italiano. Comí pasta con pollo y salsa de tomate.

¿Qué hiciste el fin de semana pasado?

Este fin de semana tengo que estudiar mucho porque tengo un examen de historia el lunes por la mañana. ¡Qué rollo! El sábado voy a ir una fiesta en la casa de mi primo Juan. Es su cumple.

¿Tienes planes para el fin de semana que viene?

SAMPLE A

This is space for extra work. Label any such extra work clearly with the question number and part.

SAMPLE B

# Junior Cycle Final Examination
# Sample Paper B

# Spanish

## Common Level

## Time: 2 hours

360 marks

| Examination number | | | | |
|---|---|---|---|---|
| | | | | |

## Instructions

There are **three** sections in this paper.

| | | | |
|---|---|---|---|
| Section A | Listening | 140 marks | 8 questions |
| Section B | Reading | 140 marks | 7 questions |
| Section C | Writing | 80 marks | 3 questions |

Answer **all** questions.

Read the instructions carefully regarding the language to be used when answering the questions.

Write your answers in the spaces provided in this booklet.

## Section A Listening 140 marks

### Question 1

Answer the following questions by putting a tick (✓) in the correct box. Tick **one** box only.

**(a)** María está en el colegio.

- verdadero ☐
- falso ☐

**(b)** ¿Qué se ha dejado en casa?

 ☐

 ☐

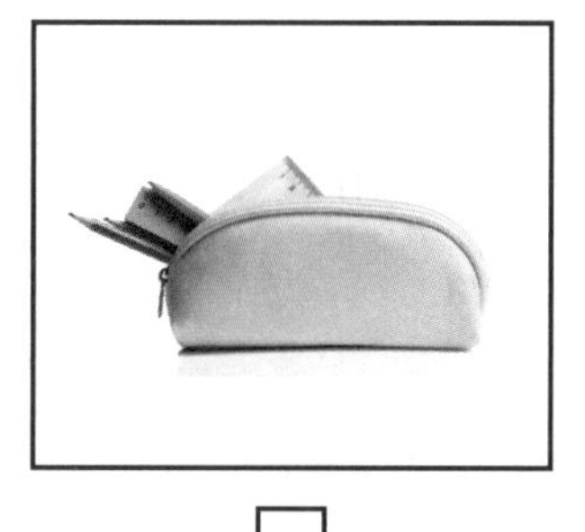 ☐

**(c)** María tiene que limpiar:

- el comedor ☐
- la cocina ☐
- su habitación ☐
- el jardín ☐

**(d)** María va a hacer la limpieza:

- mañana ☐
- esta tarde ☐
- este fin de semana ☐
- el martes que viene ☐

SAMPLE B

**Question 2**

An estate agent is advertising an apartment for rent. Tick (✓) the correct boxes.

**(a)** ¿En qué planta está el apartamento? Marca **una** con un tick (✓).

| | |
|---|---|
| la primera planta | ☐ |
| la segunda planta | ☐ |
| la tercera planta | ☐ |
| la cuarta planta | ☐ |

**(b)** El apartamento está al lado:

| | |
|---|---|
| de la piscina | ☐ |
| del cine | ☐ |
| del ayuntamiento | ☐ |
| de la playa | ☐ |

**(c)** Marca **cuatro** habitaciones que hay en el apartamento.

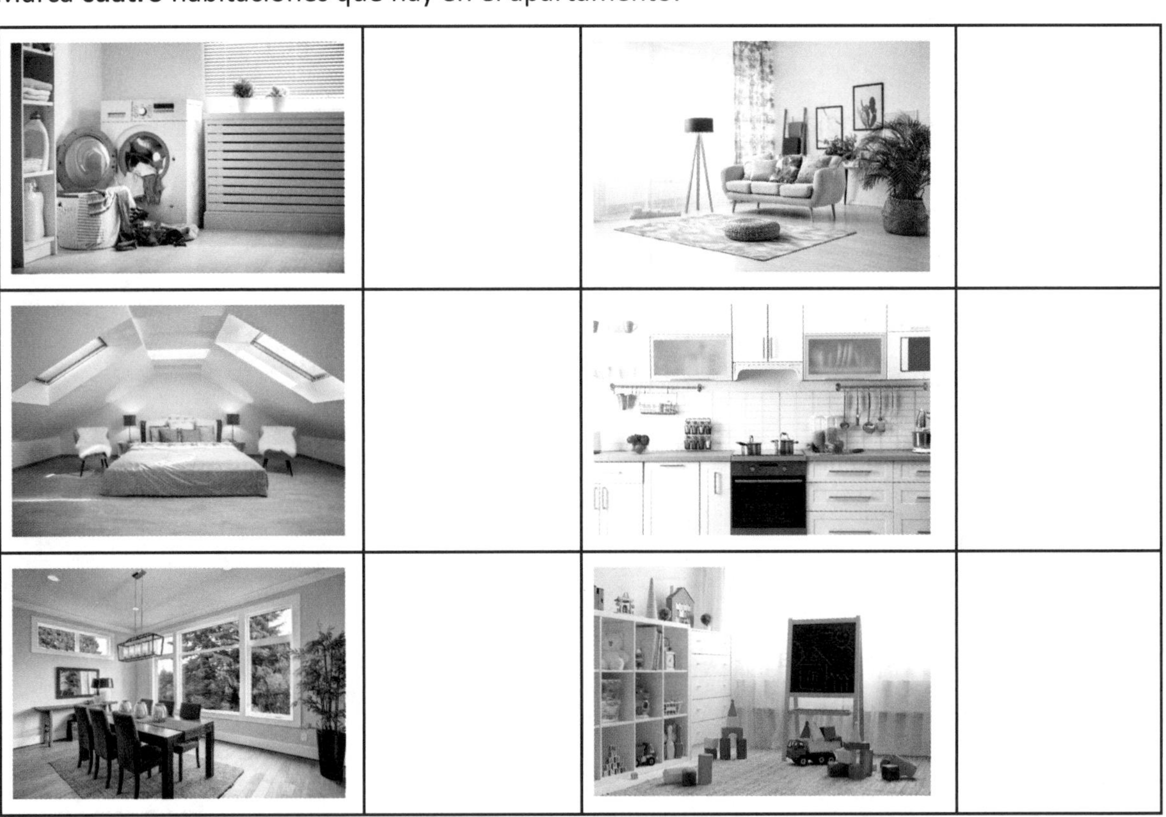

zlwvkk
Visit www.e-xamit.ie

**Question 3**

Ignacio describes how he spent last Saturday. Answer the questions **in Spanish**.

**(a)** Ignacio desayunó en casa el sábado.

verdadero ☐

falso ☐

**(b)** Marca **tres** cosas que hizo Ignacio el sábado.

| | |
|---|---|
| Fue con su padre a comprar un móvil. | |
| Comió una hamburguesa. | |
| Fue con su padre a comprar el periódico. | |
| Preparó una paella con su padre. | |
| Leyó un libro. | |
| Charló con su amiga. | |

**(c)** ¿Quién vino a su casa? Menciona **dos** parientes.

**(d)** ¿A qué hora fue al cine?

**Question 4**

Ana is talking to her coach. Answer the questions **in English**.

**(a)** What part of her body did Ana hurt?

**(b)** What was she doing when she hurt herself?

**(c)** Who will collect her and when?

| WHO | WHEN |
| --- | --- |
| | |

nmwrzn
Visit www.e-xamit.ie

**Question 5**

Antonio calls Clara. Answer the questions **in English**.

**(a)** Antonio asks Clara about the homework for what subject?

**(b)** On what page is the homework that Antonio should do?

**(c)** When is their exam?

| DAY | TIME |
| --- | --- |
| | |

expdey
Visit www.e-xamit.ie

**Question 6**

You will hear a conversation in a restaurant. Answer the questions **in English**.

**(a)** What does the man order as a starter?

|  |
|---|
|  |

**(b)** According to the **waitress** what ingredients can be found in the paella? Tick (✓) **five** of the following.

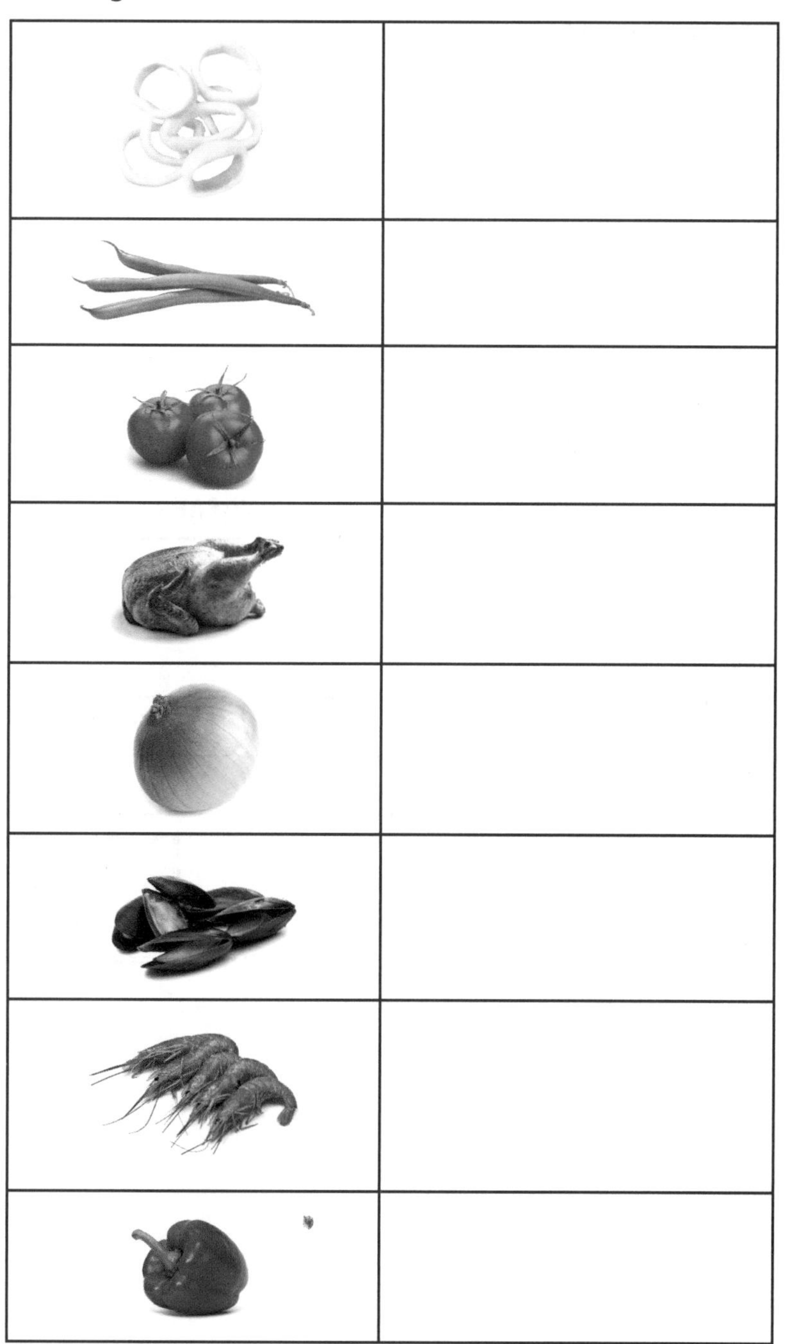

**(c)** What does the man order to drink?

|  |
|---|
|  |

gjzmoz
Visit www.e-xamit.ie

SAMPLE B

**Question 7**

You will hear a description of the famous Spanish architect Antoni Gaudí. Answer the questions **in English**.

**(a)** When was Gaudí born?

| DATE | MONTH | YEAR |
|---|---|---|
| | | |

**(b)** What did he spend a lot of time observing? Give **two** details.

| |
|---|
| |
| |

**(c)** What did he study in Barcelona?

| |
|---|
| |

**(d)** What is the Sagrada Familia and where is it?

| WHAT | WHERE |
|---|---|
| | |

**(e)** When did Gaudí die tragically?

| DATE | MONTH | YEAR |
|---|---|---|
| | | |

**Question 8**

You will hear some information about Galicia. Answer the question **in English**.

**(a)** Where exactly is Galicia situated?

**(b)** Why is it said to be like Ireland? Give **two** details.

**(c)** What is the most popular sport in Galicia?

**(d)** Why do people visit the city of Santiago de Compostela? Give **two** reasons.

**(e)** Name **three** ways you can do the Camino de Santiago.

**(f)** Name **three** foods that you can enjoy in the restaurants.



SAMPLE B

**Question 9**

Match the person's job with their place of work by filling in the grid.

| | |
|---|---|
| **A** Contable | **1** Una comisaría |
| **B** Médico | **2** Un restaurante |
| **C** Granjero | **3** Una oficina |
| **D** Profesor | **4** Un avión |
| **E** Policía | **5** Un hospital |
| **F** Camarero | **6** Una farmacia |
| **G** Auxiliar de vuelo | **7** Un instituto |
| **H** Farmacéutico | **8** Una granja |

| Letra | Número |
|---|---|
| A | |
| B | |
| C | |
| D | |
| E | |
| F | |
| G | |
| H | 6 |

**Question 10**

Look at the images below and match the correct number with the **Spanish** phrase.

| | Número |
|---|---|
| La cuenta, por favor. | |
| ¿Por dónde se va al Museo de Historia? | |
| ¿Cuánto cuestan los zapatos? | |
| Quiero una barra de pan y tres cruasanes. | |
| Está lloviendo mucho. | |
| Me he roto el tobillo. | |

SAMPLE B

nxecxf
Visit www.e-xamit.ie

**Question 11**

Read the notice and answer the questions **in Spanish**.

**Clases de natación para adultos**

Lunes, martes y miércoles de 10 a 11

12€ la clase

Entrada libre todos los días: de 16 a 20

**(a)** ¿En qué días hay clases de natación para adultos?

**(b)** ¿A qué hora empiezan las clases?

**(c)** ¿Cuánto cuesta una clase?

**(d)** ¿Cuándo hay entrada libre?

**Question 12**

Read the text and answer the questions **in Spanish**.

¡Hola! Me llamo Pablo y soy profesor de música en un instituto de secundaria. Nací en España el diecisiete de marzo de mil novecientos noventa y tres.

Soy alto y tengo los ojos marrones y el pelo castaño. Soy deportista, creativo y hablador. Toco la guitarra y la batería.

Estudié en la Universidad de Salamanca. Me gustó mucho la vida universitaria y me lo pasé fenomenal porque conocí a mucha gente e hice muchos amigos. Ahora trabajo en Badajoz y disfruto mucho dando clases a mis alumnos. Este verano quiero ir a practicar mi francés a Lyon. Tengo unos amigos allí y voy a ir a visitarlos.



**(a)** ¿Cuál es el trabajo de Pablo?

**(b)** ¿En qué año nació?

**(c)** ¿Cómo es su personalidad?

**(d)** ¿Qué instrumentos toca?

**(e)** ¿Dónde estudió?

**(f)** ¿Qué quiere hacer este verano?

**Question 13**

Miguel asks online for advice on what subjects to choose at school. Read the forum and answer the questions **in English**.

@Miguel: ¡Hola chicos! Necesito consejos. Tengo que elegir asignaturas para el año que viene pero no tengo ni idea. ¿Qué asignaturas os gustan y por qué?

@Sara: Yo elegí Dibujo y para mí es la asignatura más interesante y menos estresante. Me encanta dibujar.

@Ignacio: ¡Hola Miguel! Yo quiero estudiar Biología, Química o Física porque te darán muchas oportunidades profesionales después del colegio.

@Luis: Estudio Alemán y Francés. Creo que es importante saber hablar otras lenguas.

@Paula: ¿Para qué quieres hacer el Bachillerato? Hay más en la vida fuera del colegio. A mí no me gustan los libros y no quiero estudiar más.

1. What subject did Sara choose?

2. Why did she choose this subject?

3. Why does Ignacio want to study science subjects?

4. Which languages does Luis study?

5. What does Paula say about school?

**Question 14**

Read the text and answer the questions **in English**.

## Nace una cría de delfín en el Zoo Aquarium de Madrid

**1.** Zoo Aquarium de Madrid celebra una nueva cría de delfín en sus instalaciones en Casa de Campo. El delfín nació el pasado viernes 14 de mayo, a mediodía, cuando Mary, una hembra de 34 años, daba a luz a una cría de delfín después de doce meses de gestación. Las dos primeras semanas de vida serán cruciales para el desarrollo de la cría. Pasados ya cuatro días desde su nacimiento, todo parece apuntar al buen estado de salud del pequeño. Según los veterinarios, el pequeño es un macho que se aproxima a los diez kilos y noventa centímetros de longitud.

**2.** Por ahora, la madre Mary da al delfín toda la nutrición que necesita pero el responsable del delfinario, Carlos de las Parras, dice que a partir de los seis meses comenzará a introducir algo de pescado en su dieta. Con el fin de preservar y fortalecer el vínculo entre madre y cría, Zoo Aquarium de Madrid ha suspendido temporalmente las exhibiciones y se limitará el acceso a la grada superior del delfinario durante las dos primeras semanas.

**3.** La llegada de este nuevo habitante acuático a la familia del delfinario del Zoo de Madrid se produce en unos meses especialmente prolíficos en el Parque, a los que ya se suman Buba, el bebé de elefante asiático que recientemente ha cumplido un año; Polpeta, la cría de hipopótamo que nació el pasado verano; Xing Bao, el pequeño oso panda (nacido el 30 de agosto de 2013); Luna, la foca gris con la que se despedía el 2013; y los nacimientos más recientes de la primavera, Gaika, el macho de gorila de costa (15 de marzo) y las dos jirafas, nacidas con cinco días de diferencia, Masai y Kenia (15 y 20 de abril).

SAMPLE B

**(a)** When exactly was the dolphin born? (paragraph 1)

| DAY | DATE | MONTH | TIME |
|---|---|---|---|
| | | | |

**(b)** How long had the mother dolphin been pregnant? (paragraph 1)

**(c)** What information did the vets give about the newborn dolphin? (paragraph 1)

**(d)** What does Carlos de las Parras say about the newborn's diet? (paragraph 2)

**(e)** Who is Buba? (paragraph 3)

**(f)** When was the baby hippo born? (paragraph 3)

**(g)** What type of animal is Luna? (paragraph 3)

**(h)** What animals were born in the spring this year? (paragraph 3)

nhppvr
Visit www.e-xamit.ie

**Question 15**

Read the text about the Cíes Islands and answer the questions **in English**.

Las islas Cíes es un archipiélago que se encuentra en el océano Atlántico frente a las costas gallegas en el noroeste de España. Las islas fueron declaradas Parque Natural en 1980 y contienen unas de las playas más hermosas del mundo, de arena fina y aguas cristalinas.

El ecosistema de las islas Cíes es uno de los más ricos del mundo con una multitud de pájaros como gaviotas, y animales como conejos o ratones y, por supuesto, arañas y escarabajos. Las islas son visitadas por una gran variedad de animales marinos como pulpos, delfines, ballenas y tortugas marinas.

La playa de las Rodas es la más grande del archipiélago, con más de un kilómetro de largo, y fue elegida la mejor playa de España en 2017. Dispone de servicios de vigilancia, socorrismo, campings y restaurantes.

Durante mucho tiempo las islas estuvieron despobladas. Durante los años 70 y 80 la gente joven empezó a ir de nuevo a la isla para acampar y poder disfrutar del sol y la playa.

**(a)** Where exactly are the Islas Cíes? Give **two** details.

**(b)** Name **two** types of bird or animal found on the islands.

**(c)** Name **two** types of sea creatures found in the waters around the islands.

**(d)** Give **two** pieces of information about Rodas beach.

**(e)** Why did young people begin to return to the islands in the 70s and 80s? Give **two** details.

SAMPLE B

| Section C | Writing | 80 marks |
|---|---|---|

**Question 16**

Complete the following sentences by inserting the correct **Spanish** phrase into the space below:

**For example:**

Yo hice la reserva en línea.

| | |
|---|---|
| **está en el corazón de Madrid** | **tendremos tiempo libre** |
| **las instalaciones deportivas** | **una chuleta de cerdo con patatas asadas** |
| **en un hotel de tres estrellas** | **tarde los fines de semana** |

**(a)** Normalmente yo me despierto ______________________.

**(b)** De segundo quiero ______________________.

**(c)** La Puerta del Sol ______________________.

**(d)** Mañana ______________________ para ir a la playa.

**(e)** Lo que más me gusta de mi colegio son ______________________.

**(f)** Me alojé ______________________ en el centro de la ciudad.

**Question 17**

You are on an exchange in Spain and you met a new friend. Write a blog **in Spanish**, giving answers to the following:

**(a)** ¿Cómo se llama tu amigo?

**(b)** ¿Cómo es físicamente?

**(c)** ¿Qué tipo de persona es?

**(d)** ¿Cuáles son sus pasatiempos?

**(e)** ¿Qué hiciste con tu amigo el fin de semana pasado?

**Mi Blog**



SAMPLE B

**Question 18**

Your Spanish pen pal Carmen has emailed you with some information about her life in Spain. Write a response **in Spanish** to her questions below:

¡Hola! ¿Cómo estás? Estoy muy ocupada porque tengo un proyecto para la clase de inglés mañana. Tengo que hacer una presentación sobre mi barrio.

¿Cómo es tu barrio?

Como ya sabes me interesan mucho los deportes así que paso mucho tiempo en el gimnasio. También paso mucho tiempo en el centro comercial con mis amigas.

¿Cuáles son las distracciones para los jóvenes en tu barrio?

Tengo suerte porque tengo un trabajo a tiempo parcial, entonces puedo gastar mi dinero en lo que quiero. Trabajo en una peluquería todos los sábados.

¿Qué haces los fines de semana normalmente?

Además de mi trabajo mis padres me dan dinero cuando ayudo con las tareas domésticas. Ayudo a preparar la cena todos los días y los domingos paso la aspiradora.

¿Qué haces para ayudar en casa?

Tienes que visitarme en agosto y puedes ver mi casa. Es una casa bastante grande y está situada en una urbanización en las afueras de Salamanca.

¿Cómo es tu casa?

El mes de junio que viene iré al piso de mis primos que está en el centro de Cádiz.

¿Qué harás el verano que viene?

Tengo que irme ahora porque tengo entrenamiento con mi equipo de fútbol, perdimos nuestro partido el fin de semana pasado.

¿Qué hiciste el fin de semana pasado?

fcuflt
Visit www.e-xamit.ie

SAMPLE B

This is space for extra work. Label any such extra work clearly with the question number and part.

# Junior Cycle Final Examination
# Sample Paper C

# Spanish

## Common Level

SAMPLE C

Time: 2 hours

360 marks

| Examination number | | | | |
|---|---|---|---|---|
| | | | | |

## Instructions

There are **three** sections in this paper.

| | | | |
|---|---|---|---|
| Section A | Listening | 140 marks | 8 questions |
| Section B | Reading | 140 marks | 7 questions |
| Section C | Writing | 80 marks | 3 questions |

Answer **all** questions.

Read the instructions carefully regarding the language to be used when answering the questions.

Write your answers in the spaces provided in this booklet.

| Section A | Listening | 140 marks |
|---|---|---|

**Question 1**

Answer the following questions by putting a tick (✓) in the correct box. Tick **one** box only.

**(a)** El joven tiene catorce años.

Verdadero ☐
Falso ☐

**(b)** ¿Qué llevaba el joven?

☐

☐

☐

**(c)** La policía lo llevó:

a su casa ☐
a su colegio ☐
a la comisaría ☐
al cine ☐

**(d)** La policía avisó a:

su madre ☐
su padre ☐
sus padres ☐
su profesor ☐

SAMPLE C

**Question 2**

You will hear an announcement about special offers from a supermarket. Tick (✓) the correct boxes.

**(a)** ¿En qué sección hay un descuento de 20%?

- carnes y pescados ☐
- fruta y verduras ☐
- panadería ☐
- artículos del hogar ☐

**(b)** Marca los **seis** productos que están rebajados hoy.

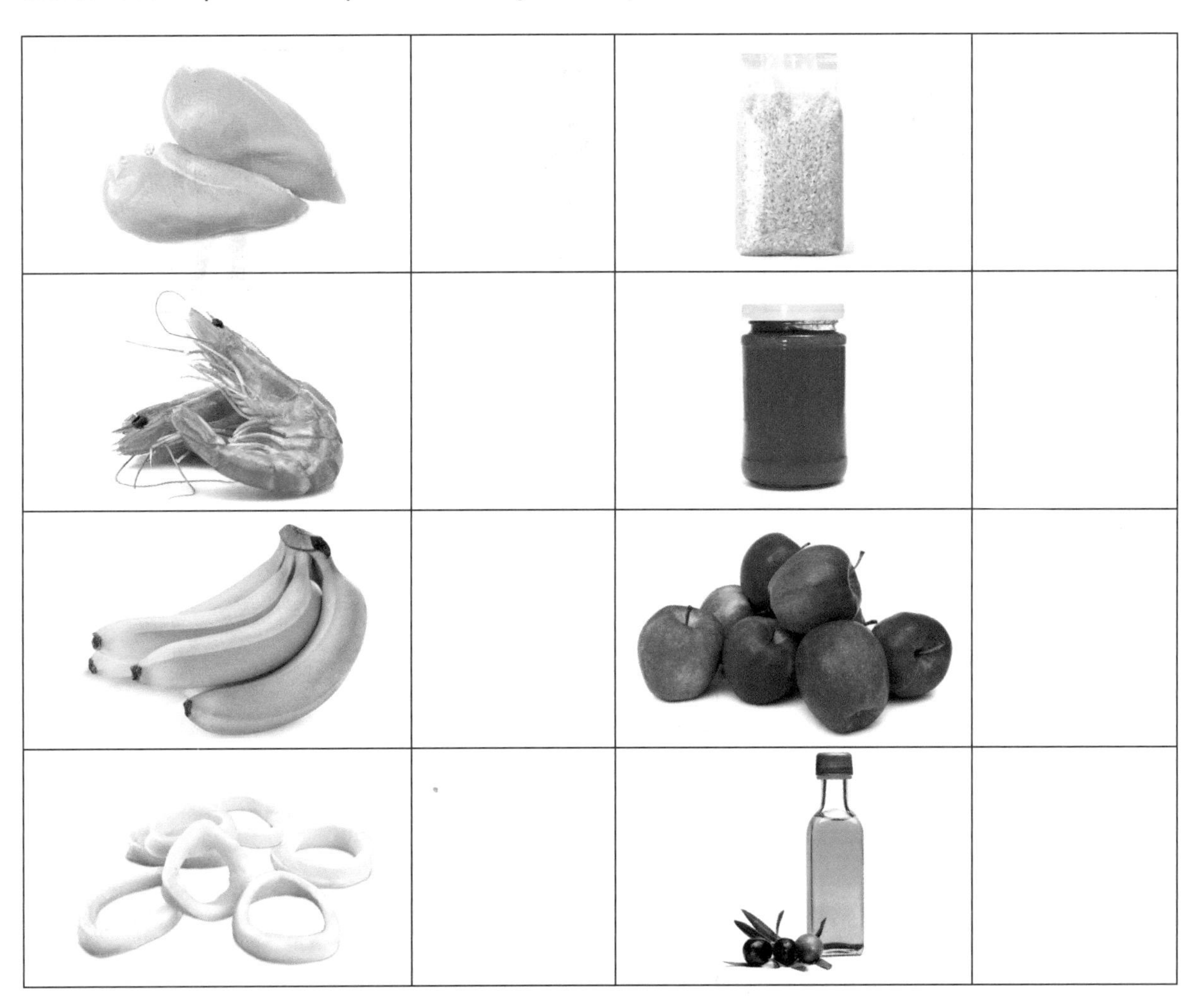

**(c)** Las ofertas terminan mañana a:

- las 7 de la mañana ☐
- las 8 de la mañana ☐
- las 7 de la tarde ☐
- las 8 de la tarde ☐

**Question 3**

You will hear an announcement from the tourist office. Answer the questions **in Spanish**.

**(a)** ¿En qué días tienen lugar las visitas guiadas?

**(b)** ¿Cuál es el precio para adultos?

- 10€ ☐
- 15€ ☐
- 20€ ☐

**(c)** ¿Cuánto tiempo dura la visita guiada?

- media hora ☐
- una hora ☐
- una hora y media ☐

**(d)** Menciona **un** producto tradicional que se puede probar.



SAMPLE C

**Question 4**

A woman is looking for directions. Answer the questions **in English**.

**(a)** What place is the woman looking for?

**(b)** What other building does the man mention?

**(c)** How does the man recommend getting there?

rvndcc
Visit www.e-xamit.ie

**Question 5**

You will hear a conversation at the bus station. Answer the questions **in English**.

**(a)** When does the next bus leave for Cádiz?

**(b)** How much does a bus ticket cost? Give **full** details.

**(c)** How many tickets does the man decide to buy?

erzvll
Visit www.e-xamit.ie

**Question 6**

You will hear a shopping centre announcement. Answer the questions **in English**.

**(a)** What departments have a 25% discount today? Tick (✓) **three** of the following.

**(b)** Name **three** items of furniture that are on offer.

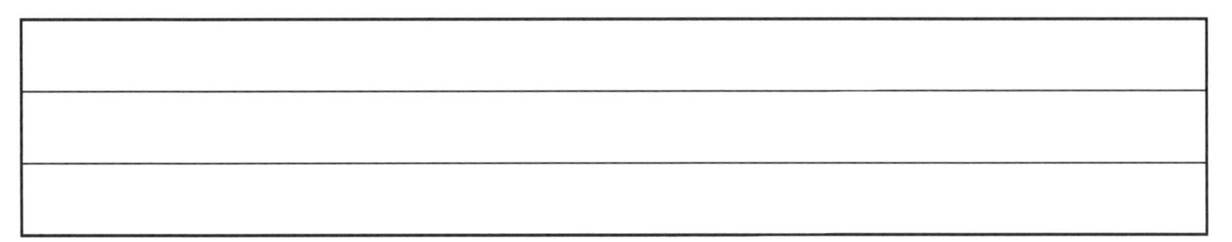

**(c)** How much do you have to spend to get free parking?

| |
|---|
| |

SAMPLE C

**Question 7**

You will hear some information about the Panama Canal. Answer the questions **in English**.

**(a)** Name **three** nationalities of explorers who identified Panama as the ideal place to build a canal.

**(b)** In what year did the building of the canal start?

**(c)** How many years did it take to build the canal?

**(d)** How long does it take boats to cross the canal?

**(e)** How long is the canal?

## Question 8

You will hear some information about the International Day of Spanish. Answer the questions **in English**.

**(a)** When was the International Day of Spanish celebrated?

**(b)** Name **four** different countries in which it was celebrated.

**(c)** How many people **study** Spanish all over the world?

**(d)** Name **two** activities that you could do as part of the celebrations.

**(e)** Name **two** ways of contacting the Instituto Cervantes in Dublin.

**(f)** Name **three** classes that the Instituto Cervantes offers.

SAMPLE C

| Section B | Reading | 140 marks |
|---|---|---|

**Question 9**

By filling in the grid, match the activity with the place in which it might take place.

| | |
|---|---|
| **A** Esquiar | **1** La discoteca |
| **B** Hacer pesas | **2** El estadio |
| **C** Leer | **3** Las montañas |
| **D** Bailar | **4** El centro comercial |
| **E** Ver un partido de fútbol | **5** El gimnasio |
| **F** Ir de compras | **6** La cocina |
| **G** El buceo | **7** El mar |
| **H** Cocinar | **8** La biblioteca |

| Letra | Número |
|---|---|
| A | |
| B | |
| C | |
| D | |
| E | |
| F | |
| G | |
| H | 6 |

**Question 10**

Look at the images below and match the correct number with the **Spanish** phrase.

| | Número |
|---|---|
| ¡Patata! Voy a sacar la foto. | |
| Entradas, por favor. | |
| Me duele la garganta. | |
| ¡Feliz año nuevo! | |
| ¡Me han comprado una bicicleta nueva! | |
| Un paquete de tiritas y un jarabe para la tos, por favor. | |

SAMPLE C

**Question 11**

Read the poster and answer the questions **in Spanish**.

# BIENVENIDOS A LA FIESTA DE SAN JUAN

## Celebra con nosotros la venida del verano con una gran fiesta en la playa

El 23 de junio en la playa Águila ven y disfruta del espectáculo de las hogueras de San Juan. El grupo flamenco Lola y Lola tocará a la medianoche.

Hay espacio acondicionado para hacer acampada. Si quieres acampar, necesitas traer saco de dormir y tienda de campaña.

No se permiten niños de menos de ocho años en la zona de acampar.

Línea de autobús: B12

Entrada gratuita.

**(a)** ¿En qué mes es la Fiesta de San Juan?

**(b)** ¿A qué hora toca el grupo flamenco Lola y Lola?

**(c)** ¿Qué línea de autobús sirve la fiesta?

**(d)** ¿Cuánto cuesta la entrada?

**Question 12**

Read the blog and answer the questions **in Spanish**.

kozgww
Visit www.e-xamit.ie

¡Hola a todos los blogueros que me seguís! Bienvenidos a mi blog.
Me llamo Lola y os cuento: Vivo en un piso en el barrio de Candilejas en Madrid. En mi barrio hay cines, y muchas tiendas de comestibles, panaderías y carnicerías. También hay bares pero no hay muchos espacios verdes. Si quiero hacer deporte tengo que coger el autobús para ir a un polideportivo que está un poco lejos de mi casa. En autobús está a diez minutos. El año pasado pusieron un huerto urbano muy chulo al lado de mi casa. El huerto te da alimentos frescos y naturales como tomates, lechuga, cebollas... Yo tengo fresas plantadas y ayudo a mis padres a regar y a cuidar del huerto. Además, cuando bajo al huerto, veo a mis amigos, charlamos, y a veces salimos por ahí a dar una vuelta.

**(a)** ¿Dónde vive Lola?

**(b)** ¿Qué hay en su barrio?

**(c)** ¿Cómo va al polideportivo?

**(d)** ¿Cuánto tiempo dura el viaje?

**(e)** ¿Cuáles son los alimentos que cultivan en el huerto?

**(f)** ¿Qué tipo de fruta está cultivando Lola?

SAMPLE C

**Question 13**

Pablo asked for advice on an online forum about whether or not he should travel to Ireland to do an English course this summer. Read the forum and answer the questions **in English**.

@Pablo: ¡Hola gente! ¿Estáis por ahí? Hoy tengo una pregunta para haceros: mis padres me obligan a hacer un curso de inglés porque he suspendido esa asignatura. El caso es que me dicen que puedo irme a Irlanda para estudiar allí este verano. Yo preferiría hacer el curso aquí en España. Yo no sé qué hacer, tengo un poco de miedo porque nunca he estado solo en otro país sin mis padres. ¿A alguien le ha pasado algo así?

@María: Hola Pablo, yo estuve en Londres con mis padres y no me gustó nada. Llovía todo el tiempo. La comida es horrible y no comprendía nada cuando la gente me hablaba.

@Margarita: Hola, pues a mí Londres sí me gustó. Me pareció un sitio muy chulo con muchos monumentos y mercadillos. Lo mejor: conoces a mucha gente y haces amigos.

@Mencía: Hola, yo estuve viviendo con una familia en Dublín. Fui sola pero lo pasé fenomenal. En la familia me trataron muy bien y me ayudaron mucho. El curso que hice me ayudó a mejorar mi inglés, sobre todo la pronunciación.

(a) Why is Pablo a bit scared to go to Ireland?

(b) Who did María go to London with?

(c) What was the weather like there?

(d) What did she think of the food there?

(e) What did Margarita like about London?

(f) What aspect of Mencía's English particularly improved during her stay in Ireland?

**Question 14**

Read the text and answer the questions **in English**.

## Ángela Ruiz Robles, inventora del prototipo de libro digital

**1.** Ángela Ruiz Robles fue una inventora española que creó el primer prototipo de libro digital en el año mil novecientos sesenta y dos. Ángela nació en León, una ciudad que está en el norte de España, en mil ochocientos noventa y cinco. Después de estudiar Magisterio en la universidad de esa ciudad, consiguió un puesto de trabajo en el Ferrol, una ciudad en el noroeste de España. Allí comenzó a trabajar como profesora y pronto descubrió que cada estudiante aprende a un ritmo diferente.

**2.** En aquella época, muchos niños no iban a la escuela porque o era muy cara o los niños tenían que trabajar y, además, asistir al colegio no era obligatorio. Ángela daba clases gratuitas algunas tardes a estos niños. Por todo esto, Ángela fue una maestra muy querida entre los alumnos y sus padres.

**3.** Ella vio que las carteras de sus alumnos pesaban mucho porque tenían que llevar muchos libros a la escuela, por lo que creó un libro que contenía todas las asignaturas. El libro tenía distintas láminas con dibujos. Cuando el alumno tocaba con el dedo la lámina, ésta se encendía y aparecía un texto para leer. También diseñó el circuito eléctrico dentro del libro para poder encender luces y sonidos. Esta "enciclopedia mecánica", como se llamó, era ligera, por lo que no se necesitaba llevar muchos libros; era portátil, se podía utilizar en casa y en el cole; y además, usar este libro hacía más atractivo e interesante el aprendizaje para los alumnos, sobre todo, para aquellos que no veían o escuchaban bien.

**4.** Por desgracia, aunque patentó su invento, no encontró ninguna compañía española para crearlo y hacerlo famoso y conocido. Habría que esperar unas décadas más para disfrutar de nuestros actuales libros digitales y tabletas.

**(a)** In what year did Ángela Ruiz Robles create the first digital book? (paragraph 1)

**(b)** Where was she born and in what year? (paragraph 1)

| WHERE | WHAT YEAR |
|---|---|
| | |

**(c)** What job did she start after finishing university? (paragraph 1)

**(d)** Why did many children not go to school at that time? (paragraph 2)

**(e)** What did Ángela do for children who could not attend school? (paragraph 2)

**(f)** What inspired Ángela to create a digital book? (paragraph 3)

**(g)** Name one advantage of the 'mechanical encyclopedia' that she created. (paragraph 3)

**(h)** Why did she never become famous? (paragraph 4)

## Question 15

Read the text about Spanish festivals and answer the questions **in English**.

**1.** En todas las zonas de España, pueblos y ciudades, se celebran fiestas patronales. Estas fiestas corresponden normalmente a un momento importante de la historia de ese lugar. La mayoría de las fiestas son de origen religioso pues se celebran en honor a un santo que ha intercedido en la vida de sus habitantes.

**2.** Una de las fiestas más imponentes y hermosas es la Fiesta de Moros y Cristianos en la localidad de Alcoy, en Alicante, que tiene lugar los días del veintidós al veinticuatro de abril. Es una fiesta que se celebra en honor a San Jorge. Es una auténtica recreación de las batallas que sucedieron de verdad en el año 1276 entre árabes ("Moros") que habitaban la zona en ese momento y los nuevos pobladores ("Cristianos") que luchaban por quedarse en el territorio. No podemos olvidar que en su historia España ha estado habitada por muchos pueblos como los romanos (por eso hay acueductos y murallas) o los árabes (por eso hay mezquitas y palacios como La Alhambra en Granada).

**3.** Los ciudadanos de Alcoy se visten como se hacía en la época medieval: algunas mujeres se disfrazan de princesas cristianas y otras de princesas árabes con velos y turbantes. Los hombres cristianos como caballeros medievales y los hombres árabes como guerreros. Todos desfilan por las calles de la ciudad: algunos a caballo y otros a pie; y al final del día hay una representación donde simulan una batalla. Por la noche, el desfile acaba con la aparición de una figura de San Jorge que pone fin a todas las celebraciones del día bajo los alegres colores de fuegos artificiales.

**(a)** What is the origin of most Spanish festivals? (paragraph 1)

**(b)** When and where exactly does the Fiesta de Moros y Cristianos take place? (paragraph 2)

**(c)** Name **one** building or monument that was built by the Arabs in Spain. (paragraph 2)

**(d)** What exactly happens during this festival in daytime? (Give **two** details). (paragraph 3)

**(e)** How does the festival end? (paragraph 3)



SAMPLE C

| Section C | Writing | 80 marks |
|---|---|---|

**Question 16**

Complete the following sentences by inserting the correct **Spanish** phrase into the space below:

**For example:**

Suelo pasar mucho tiempo **en la casa de mi amigo**.

| | |
|---|---|
| **comprar un vestido** | **El año pasado** |
| **para ver la nueva película** | **sitios de interés** |
| **las normas ridículas** | **el sábado por la noche** |

**(a)** ¿Quieres venir a mi fiesta ______________________________?

**(b)** Voy al cine ______________________________ del Hombre Araña.

**(c)** Tengo que ______________________________ para mi fiesta de cumpleaños.

**(d)** Hay muchos ______________________________ en mi barrio

**(e)** ______________________________ hice un intercambio en España.

**(f)** Lo peor del colegio son ______________________________.

**Question 17**

You are on an exchange in Córdoba with the González family. Write a blog **in Spanish**, giving answers to the following:

**(a)** ¿Cómo es la familia?

**(b)** ¿Cómo es la ciudad?

**(c)** ¿Cómo es la casa de la familia González?

**(d)** ¿Qué hiciste la semana pasada?

**(e)** ¿Cuáles son tus planes para este fin de semana?

**Mi Blog**

SAMPLE C

**Question 18**

Your Spanish friend Joaquín has emailed you with some information about himself and his life in Spain. Write a response **in Spanish** to his questions below:

¿Qué pasa? Todo me va bien a mí. Mi madre me ha dicho que puedo invitarte a nuestra casa en junio. Espero que puedas venir porque vamos a ir a nuestro piso en Málaga este verano. Normalmente vamos a la playa y nadamos en el mar casi todos los días.

¿Qué sueles hacer en el verano?

Me encanta el clima en Málaga en el verano. Hace calor y sol todo el tiempo.

¿Cómo es el clima en Irlanda?

El verano pasado hicimos una excursión a Nerja, un pueblo que está bastante cerca de Málaga. Fuimos a ver El Balcón de Europa, un sitio donde hay vistas maravillosas. Comimos en un restaurante cerca de la playa. Comí tortilla española y gambas.

¿Cómo es la comida en Irlanda?

Un día hicimos esquí acuático y vela. Me encantan los deportes.

¿Te interesan los deportes?

Conocí a una chica súper simpática allí también. Es irlandesa como tú. Se llama Clíona y tiene quince años. Practicaba mi inglés con ella. Me encanta hablar en inglés pero la verdad es que detesto la gramática y los verbos.

¿Qué cosas te gustan de aprender español?

El año que viene quiero visitar Irlanda y hacer un intercambio allí para mejorar mi inglés.

¿Cuáles son las cosas más interesantes que debo hacer cuando vaya a Irlanda?

Tengo que irme ahora porque he quedado con mi amiga Ana en el cine a las ocho. Vamos a ver una comedia.

¿Qué haces con tus amigos normalmente?

This is space for extra work. Label any such extra work clearly with the question number and part.

Junior Cycle Final Examination
Sample Paper D

# Spanish

Common Level

Time: 2 hours

360 marks

| Examination number | | | | |
|---|---|---|---|---|
| | | | | |

SAMPLE D

# Instructions

There are **three** sections in this paper.

| | | | |
|---|---|---|---|
| Section A | Listening | 140 marks | 8 questions |
| Section B | Reading | 140 marks | 7 questions |
| Section C | Writing | 80 marks | 3 questions |

Answer **all** questions.

Read the instructions carefully regarding the language to be used when answering the questions.

Write your answers in the spaces provided in this booklet.

| Section A | Listening | 140 marks |
|---|---|---|

**Question 1**

Listen to the advertisement and answer the following questions **in Spanish**.

**(a)** ¿En qué día comienzan los cursos?

**(b)** ¿Cuál es la duración mínima de los cursos?

- un fin de semana ☐
- una semana ☐
- un año ☐

**(c)** ¿Cuál es el horario de las clases?

- 17h – 20h ☐
- 17h – 21h ☐
- 18h – 20h ☐
- 18h – 21h ☐

**(d)** ¿Qué hacen los alumnos al final de cada curso?

**Question 2**

You will hear Pedro's mother explaining Pedro's absence from school. Answer the questions below **in English**.

**(a)** Who is Francisco Ramírez?

**(b)** When is Pedro's hospital appointment?

**(c)** Why does Pedro have to go to hospital? Give **full** details.

**(d)** How long will it take him to recover?

**(e)** When will Pedro return to school?

## Question 3

Listen to Antonio tell a story and answer the questions by putting a tick (✓) in the correct box. Tick **one** box only.

**(a)** ¿Cuándo vio Antonio el anuncio?

- el lunes pasado ☐
- el martes pasado ☐
- la semana pasada ☐
- el año pasado ☐

**(b)** El perro es un collie de pelo negro y es muy grande.

- verdadero ☐
- falso ☐

**(c)** ¿Qué hacía Antonio cuando vio el perro?

- iba a girar a la izquierda ☐
- iba a girar a la derecha ☐
- iba a cruzar el semáforo ☐

**(d)** ¿Quién llamó a los dueños del perro?

- su padre ☐
- su abuelo ☐
- su madre ☐
- su primo ☐

**Question 4**

Listen to the weather forecast and answer the questions below **in English**.

**(a)** Is Winter mentioned?

**(b)** For what day and date is this weather forecast?

| DAY | DATE |
|---|---|
| | |

**(c)** What are the maximum and minimum temperatures expected?

| MINIMUM TEMPERATURE | MAXIMUM TEMPERATURE |
|---|---|
| | |

**(d)** What are motorists asked to do? Give **one** detail.

## Question 5

Listen to Jaime talking about a summer camp and answer the questions below **in English**.

**(a)** Where is San Sebastián?

**(b)** *Los pinxtos* are:

**(c)** What is the weather usually like in San Sebastián?

**(d)** *La pelota* is:

- a traditional food ☐
- a Basque song ☐
- an area in San Sebastián ☐
- a Basque sport ☐

SAMPLE D

**Question 6**

Listen to the description of the Dunes of Corrubedo Natural Park and answer the following questions **in English**.

**(a)** Name **two** things that you can see in the park.

|  |
|---|
|  |

**(b)** How many different walking routes are there in the park?

|  |
|---|

**(c)** Write any **two** of the park rules.

|  |
|---|
|  |

**Question 7**

Listen to the **three** news items and answer the questions **in English**.

**(a)** What advice is given to students starting their exams in the next two weeks?

**(b)** What caused the death of two people in Seville?

**(c)** What nationality is the player who scored the goal for Real Madrid?

SAMPLE D

**Question 8**

Listen to the announcement and answer the questions below **in English**.

**(a)** What date is it?

**(b)** Which sports team won the match yesterday?

**(c)** When is the no uniform day?

**(d)** What will the money raised from the no uniform day be used for?

**(e)** Mention **three** extra-curricular activities that will take place this evening.

| Section B | Reading | 140 marks |
|---|---|---|

**Question 9**

Match the following words and images by filling in the grid.

| | | | |
|---|---|---|---|
| **A.** | La heladería | **1.** | |
| **B.** | Facturación de maletas | **2.** | |
| **C.** | El parque de atracciones | **3.** | |
| **D.** | Riesgo de nieve | **4.** | |
| **E.** | La librería | **5.** | |
| **F.** | Semáforos | **6.** | |
| **G.** | Se alquilan tumbonas | **7.** | |
| **H.** | Prohibido fumar | **8.** | |
| **I.** | El albergue juvenil | **9.** | |
| **J.** | Albóndigas | **10.** | |

| LETRA | NÚMERO |
|---|---|
| A. | |
| B. | |
| C. | |
| D. | |
| E. | |
| F. | |
| G. | 2 |
| H. | |
| I. | |
| J. | |

SAMPLE D

**Question 10**

Read the advertisements below and match the correct letter to the theme in the grid.

**A.**

**Servicio de fontanería**
Arreglamos filtraciones, desatascamos tuberías
Todas las áreas de Málaga cubiertas
Teléfono: 624272159

**B.**

Aprende bachata, chachachá
Únete a nuestros profesores y sé un experto en bailes de salón
Tráete los tacones de casa
Calle Rincón 57
Teléfono: 958391204

**C.**

**RELOJERÍA** taller de reparaciones Rogelio
Reparamos todo tipo de relojes: de pulsera, de pared, de cuco; modernos y antiguos
También cambiamos pilas
Servicio garantizado

**D.**

Bienvenidos a nuestra biblioteca municipal
Horario: 8:00-20:00
Para préstamos: 8:30-19:30
Código wifi: biblioteca00
Avenida de la Palmera, 47

**E.**

**CONSERVATORIO MUNICIPAL RUPERTO CHAPÍ**
Damos clases de todos los instrumentos
Cursos de dirección de orquesta
HORARIO DE ATENCIÓN AL PÚBLICO: 16:30-19:00
www.conservatoriochapi.com

F.

Fiestas patronales
Fiestas en honor a Santiago Apóstol
22-28 de julio

G.

**PASTELERÍA EL PETISÚ**
Prueba nuestros deliciosos tocinos de cielo,
brazo de gitano y bocaditos de nata
Se hacen tartas por encargo para bodas,
bautizos, comuniones y cumpleaños
Puedes disfrutar dentro en nuestros salones
o si lo prefieres puedes llevarlo para comer en casa

H.

Servicio de limpieza
Limpieza de portería
Limpiezas de hogar
Mantenimiento de jardines
Teléfono: 956 747488
Presupuesto gratis y sin compromiso

| Letra | Tema |
|---|---|
| | Ballroom dancing lessons |
| | A library |
| | A religious festival |
| | Cleaning services |
| | Plumbing services |
| | A bakery |
| E | A music school |
| | Watch repairs |

**Question 11**

Read the postcard and answer the questions **in Spanish**.

| | |
|---|---|
| **Madrid, 2 de marzo**<br><br>**Querido abuelo:**<br><br>**Estoy en Madrid con mis compañeros de clase. Hoy hemos ido al zoo en la Casa de Campo. Hemos visto un montón de animales: elefantes, jirafas, leones, rinocerontes y mis favoritos, los monos. Estamos alojados en un albergue juvenil, en el centro de la ciudad. Mañana por la mañana iremos al Palacio Real. Tengo muchas ganas de verlo. Dile hola a la abuela.**<br><br>**Besos,**<br><br>**Yolanda** | **Antonio González Cruz**<br>**C/ San Basilio 3º A**<br>**Alicante,**<br>**España**<br>**03007** |

**(a)** ¿Qué mes es?

**(b)** ¿Dónde está Yolanda?

**(c)** ¿Dónde ha ido hoy?

**(d)** ¿Cuándo irá al Palacio Real?

**Question 12**

Read María José's blog and answer the questions **in Spanish**.

¡Hola, blogueros! Bienvenidos a mi blog. Me llamo María José pero todos me llaman Emejo, es mi apodo. Soy de Cuenca, que es una ciudad muy pequeña en el centro de España, pero vivo en Valladolid, en una casa muy bonita de dos plantas. Valladolid también es una ciudad muy pequeña, así que puedes ir andando a todos los sitios. Tengo un hermano más pequeño que va a la escuela de primaria. Yo empiezo este año primero de bachiller. Mis asignaturas preferidas son la historia y la geografía. No me gustan nada las asignaturas de ciencias como la biología o las matemáticas. En mi tiempo libre me gusta quedar con amigos, ¡tengo muchos! ☺ y jugar al baloncesto. ¡Soy muy alta y juego muy bien!

**(a)** ¿Dónde está Cuenca?

**(b)** ¿Cómo es la casa de María José?

**(c)** ¿Cómo es Valladolid?

**(d)** ¿Cuántos hermanos tiene María José?

**(e)** ¿Cuáles son sus asignaturas favoritas?

**(f)** ¿Qué deporte practica María José?



SAMPLE D

## Question 13

Mary asks an online forum for advice on what to wear to an event. Read the forum and answer the questions **in English**.

@Mary: ¡Hola a todos! Una pregunta. Este mes tengo la boda de mi prima y necesito ponerme algo formal. A mí me encantan los vaqueros, leggings y camisetas, pero mi madre dice que ni hablar, que tengo que llevar otra cosa. ¿Qué pensáis: pantalones, vestidos, faldas? #AYUDAboda

@Jessica: Yo me compré un vestido para el cumpleaños de mi hermana. Creo que es muy elegante y puedes usarlo para otras fiestas.

@Pablo: A mí no me gusta ir a ninguna celebración formal, son muy aburridas y hay mucha gente. ¿No puedes quedarte en casa?

@Sonsoles: Pues a mí los vestidos me resultan muy incómodos, yo creo que llevar pantalones y una blusa bonita puede ser una buena opción.

**(a)** What event is Mary going to this month?

**(b)** What three types of clothing does Mary usually like to wear?

**(c)** What item of clothing did Jessica buy?

**(d)** What occasion did Jessica buy the new outfit for?

**(e)** Why does Pablo not like formal occasions?

**(f)** What does Sonsoles recommend that Mary should wear?

## Question 14

Read the text about Lionel Messi and answer the questions **in Spanish**.

Lionel Messi es un futbolista argentino que nació el 24 de junio de 1987 en Rosario. Tiene dos hermanos mayores y una hermana menor. En el año 1992, cuando tenía cinco años, su abuela lo motivó a dedicarse al fútbol y empezó su formación como futbolista en el club Abanderado Grandoli. Muy pronto empezó a dar muestra de su gran talento. El 17 de septiembre de 2000 viajó a Barcelona con su padre para buscar un futuro como futbolista. En Barcelona jugó un partido de prueba con el equipo infantil A del Club de Fútbol de Barcelona. Fue un comienzo exitoso ya que marcó seis goles. El 14 de diciembre de 2000 sus padres y su agente firmaron un acuerdo con F.C. Barcelona sobre una servilleta de papel. Messi jugó con los equipos menores del Barcelona entre 2000 y 2005. Debutó con el primer equipo en noviembre del año 2003. Está considerado el mejor jugador del mundo. Con el F.C. Barcelona ganó diez títulos de La Liga y cuatro títulos de la Liga de Campeones y es el primer futbolista en la historia que ha ganado cinco veces el Balón de Oro. Desde 2021 juega con el F.C. Paris-Saint-Germain.

**(a)** When was Lionel Messi born?

**(b)** What age was he when he started playing football?

**(c)** His grandmother encouraged him to get involved in football.

True ☐ False ☐

**(d)** Who traveled to Barcelona with him?

**(e)** How do we know that his test match with the youth team was a success?

**(f)** What happened in November 2003?

**(g)** What great achievements has he had as a footballer?

SAMPLE D

**Question 15**

Read the recipe below and answer the questions **in English**.

Si quieres una comida sana, saludable y casera, aquí tienes nuestra receta de lujo:

**FILETES DE POLLO EMPANADOS**

**Tiempo:** Cuarenta y cinco minutos

**Ingredientes (para dos personas):**
4 pechugas de pollo
Pan rallado
2 dientes de ajo
Perejil
1 huevo
Sal
Aceite de girasol para freír

**Utensilios:**
Un bol grande
Un plato
Una sartén
Dos bandejas

**Instrucciones:**

1. Compra pechugas de pollo. Si son muy gruesas, córtalas en filetes por la mitad. Los filetes tienen que ser delgados y planos.
2. Pon sal.
3. Bate el huevo en el bol grande y añade el perejil y el ajo muy, muy picados.
4. Pon las pechugas de pollo dentro del bol y déjalas en remojo unos minutos.
5. En el plato pon el pan rallado.
6. Coge la pechuga de pollo remojada en huevo, colócala en el plato y cúbrela de pan rallado.
7. Pon la sartén al fuego con aceite.
8. Cuando el aceite esté caliente, añade las pechugas de pollo a la sartén y fríelas.
9. Dalas vueltas en la sartén hasta que los dos lados estén dorados.
10. Sácalas, ¡y buen provecho!
11. Sírvelas con mayonesa o salsa de tomate, acompañadas de patatas fritas y una ensalada mixta.

**(a)** How long does it take to prepare this recipe?

**(b)** How many people is this recipe for?

**(c)** Apart from chicken, name **three** ingredients in this recipe.

**(d)** Name **three** utensils needed to cook this recipe.

**(e)** According to step 1 of the recipe, what should you do to the chicken fillets if they are very thick?

**(f)** According to step 8, when should you add the chicken to the pan?

**(g)** According to step 11, how should you serve the chicken? (Give **full** details.)

| Section C | Writing | 80 marks |
|---|---|---|

**Question 16**

Josh wants to do a Spanish course in a language school in Salamanca. Fill in the form **in Spanish** to register for the course using the details below.

Josh Healy lives at 132 Riverside View, Glenanail, County Galway and his date of birth is 13 September 2006. His email address is jshealy06@mailer.com and his mobile number is 086 1306 295. He is travelling to Salamanca to do a Spanish course from 12–26 June. He speaks basic Spanish and wants to do an intensive course and stay with a family in a single room on full board.

| INFORMACIÓN DEL CURSO | DATOS DEL ALUMNO |
|---|---|
| Número de semanas: ☐ | Nombre: ☐ |
| Fecha de llegada: ☐ | Apellido: ☐ |
| Fecha de salida: ☐ | Fecha de nacimiento: ☐ |
| **Tipo de curso:** Clases particulares ☐ | Dirección: ☐ |
| Curso intensivo ☐ | Ciudad/Pueblo: ☐ |
| Programa para profesores de español ☐ | País de residencia: ☐ |
| **Alojamiento:** Residencia estudiantil ☐ | Número de teléfono: ☐ |
| Apartamento compartido ☐ | Correo electrónico: ☐ |
| Con familia ☐ | |
| **Habitación:** Individual ☐ | **Nivel de español:** Básico ☐ |
| Doble ☐ | Intermedio ☐ |
| **Comidas:** Alojamiento y desayuno ☐ | Avanzado ☐ |
| Media pensión ☐ | |
| Pensión completa ☐ | |

## Question 17

It's your birthday and you are going to have a party in your house. Complete the following text message conversation **in Spanish** inviting Sara to the party.

**(a)** Ask Sara if she would like to come to your birthday party.

**(b)** Say that the party is on Saturday 5 July at 8pm in your house.

**(c)** Say that you have bought hamburgers and sausages for a barbeque.

**(d)** Say that your sister is going to make a cake.

**(e)** Describe what you will wear for the party.

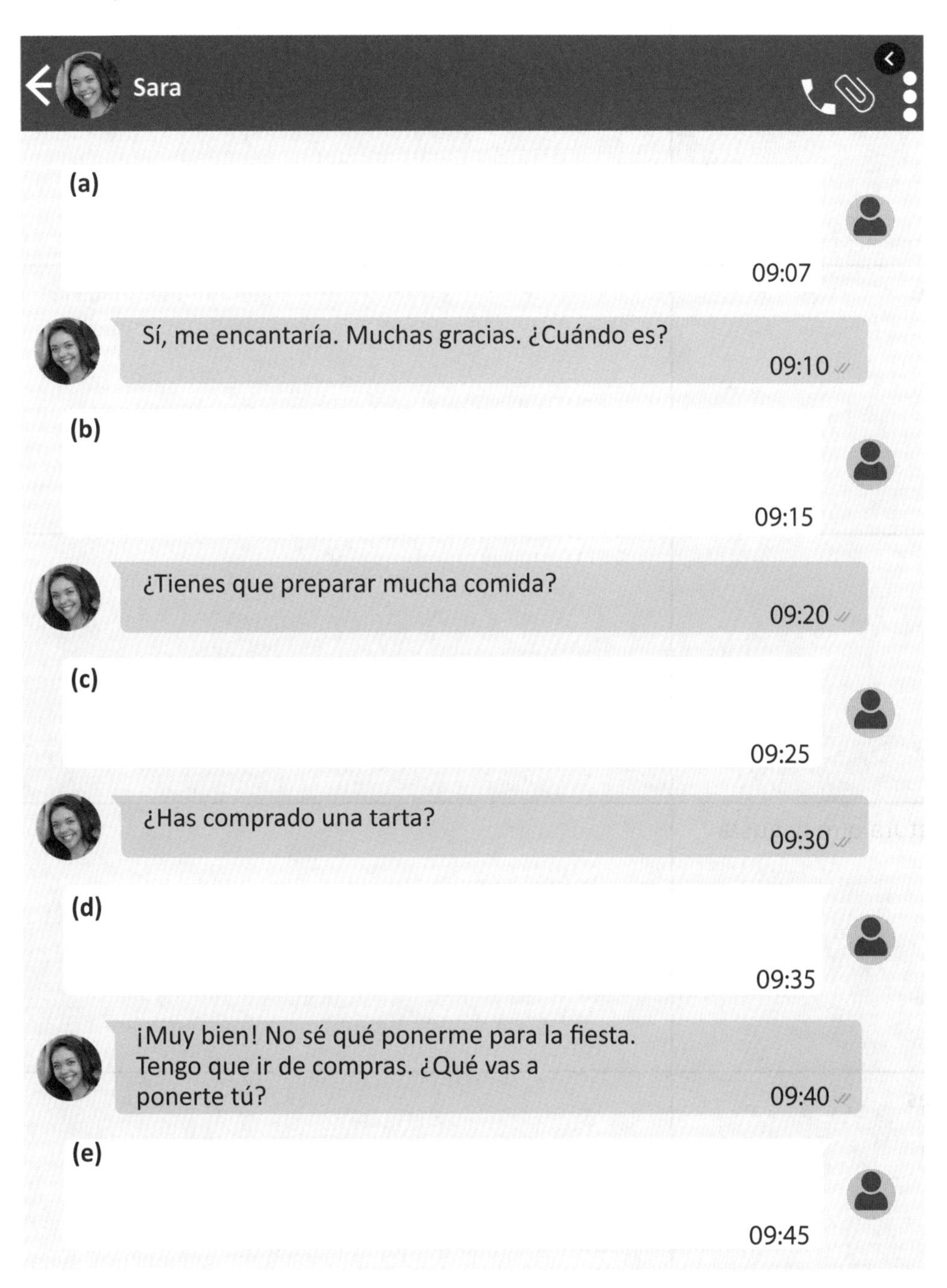


SAMPLE D

**Question 18**

You have to write a description of your secondary school for a magazine. Fill in each row in the grid with **two** complete sentences **in Spanish**.

| | |
|---|---|
| Tu instituto | |
| Los profesores | |
| El uniforme | |
| Las reglas | |
| Una asignatura que te gusta | |
| Los deberes | |

This is space for extra work. Label any such extra work clearly with the question number and part.

Junior Cycle Final Examination
Sample Paper E

# Spanish

Common Level

Time: 2 hours

360 marks

| Examination number | | | | |
|---|---|---|---|---|
| | | | | |

SAMPLE E

## Instructions

There are **three** sections in this paper.

| | | | |
|---|---|---|---|
| Section A | Listening | 140 marks | 8 questions |
| Section B | Reading | 140 marks | 7 questions |
| Section C | Writing | 80 marks | 3 questions |

Answer **all** questions.

Read the instructions carefully regarding the language to be used when answering the questions.

Write your answers in the spaces provided in this booklet.

| Section A | Listening | 140 marks |
|---|---|---|

**Question 1**

Listen to Susana talking about an exchange and answer the questions below by putting a tick (✓) under the correct image.

**(a)** ¿Qué tiempo hacía durante su intercambio?

☐ ☐ ☐ ☐

**(b)** ¿Qué le pareció interesante?

☐ ☐ ☐ ☐

**(c)** ¿Qué le gustó de la comida irlandesa?

☐ ☐ ☐ ☐

**(d)** ¿Qué se come más en España que en Irlanda?

☐ ☐ ☐ ☐

**Question 2**

Listen to the advertisement and answer the questions below **in Spanish.**

**(a)** Menciona **una** actividad que se puede hacer durante la excursión.

[ ]

**(b)** ¿Cuál es la capacidad máxima del barco?

5 personas ☐

6 personas ☐

7 personas ☐

**(c)** ¿Cuánto tiempo duran los viajes más largos?

4 horas ☐

8 horas ☐

18 horas ☐

**(d)** Completa el número de teléfono.

9 _____ _____ 64 57 _____ _____

**Question 3**

Listen to the voice message and answer the questions **in Spanish**.

**(a)** ¿Cuánto cuesta la reparación?

**(b)** Completa el número de teléfono de la tienda de reparación.

987 __ __ 67 __ __

**(c)** ¿A qué hora está abierta la tienda de lunes a viernes?

De ________ a ________ por la mañana y de ________ a ________ por la tarde.

SAMPLE E

**Question 4**

Listen to the advertisement and answer the questions by putting a tick (✓) in the correct box.
Tick **one** box only.

**(a)** ¿Masterchef Junior es para niños de cuántos años?

- 8 – 10 años ☐
- 8 – 12 años ☐
- 10 – 12 años ☐
- 12 – 18 años ☐

**(b)** Para participar, tus padres deben:

- llamar a la oficina ☐
- describir un menú ☐
- completar un formulario en línea ☐

**(c)** ¿Qué debe incluir el menú?

- un plato, un postre y una bebida ☐
- dos platos y un postre ☐
- dos platos y una bebida ☐

**(d)** Es una gran oportunidad para hacer nuevos amigos y aprender más sobre la comida.

- verdadero ☐
- falso ☐

## Question 5

Listen to the weather forecast and answer the following questions **in English**.

**(a)** What date is the weather forecast for?

**(b)** Fill in the grid with **one** detail about the weather forecast in each region.

| REGION | FORECAST |
|---|---|
| The centre of the country | |
| Catalonia | |

**(c)** In Galicia they are expecting maximum temperatures of ________________ degrees and minimum temperatures of ________________ degrees.

## Question 6

Listen to the announcement on the metro and answer the questions **in English**.

**(a)** What colour is line 1?

**(b)** On what dates will this Metro line not run?

**(c)** How many special bus services are there?

SAMPLE E

**Question 7**

Listen to the news report and answer the questions **in English**.

**(a)** How many passengers were evacuated from the cruise ship?

**(b)** Where was the cruise ship coming from?

**(c)** On what date did the incident happen?

**(d)** What were the most serious outcomes of the incident? Mention at least one outcome.

## Question 8

Listen to the presentation about Lanzarote and answer the questions **in English**.

**(a)** Where is Lanzarote situated?

**(b)** What information is given about the climate in Lanzarote? Mention at least one detail.

**(c)** How was Lanzarote formed?

**(d)** Name one geographical feature that tourists particularly like to visit.

**(e)** What is the Aloe Vera plant used for? Mention at least one detail.

| Section B | Reading | 140 marks |
|---|---|---|

**Question 9**

Match the following words and images by filling in the grid.

| | |
|---|---|
| **A.** El laboratorio de ciencias | **1.**  |
| **B.** Palomitas | **2.**  |
| **C.** El comedor | **3.**  |
| **D.** Club de paracaídismo | **4.**  |
| **E.** La catedral | **5.**  |
| **F.** Facturación | **6.**  |
| **G.** La entrada | **7.**  |
| **H.** Prohibido aparcar | **8.**  |
| **I.** La comisaría | **9.**  |
| **J.** Escuela | **10.**  |

| LETRA | NÚMERO |
|---|---|
| A. | |
| B. | |
| C. | |
| D. | 7 |
| E. | |
| F. | |
| G. | |
| H. | |
| I. | |
| J. | |

## Question 10

Read the online forum below and answer the questions that follow **in Spanish**.

Bilbao, 10 de mayo

Querida Leticia:

Estoy en Bilbao con mi equipo de vóleibol. Jugaremos en un torneo contra otros equipos mañana. Desafortunadamente hace mucho frío y está lloviendo, pero estamos alojados en un hotel cerca del centro de la ciudad y hay una piscina cubierta. El domingo por la mañana vamos a visitar el famoso museo Guggenheim antes de volver a Granada. Bueno, me tengo que ir.

Besos,

Javi

Leticia Sánchez Rodríguez

C/ San Basilio 309

Granada,

España

18013

**(a)** ¿Qué mes es?

**(b)** ¿Dónde esta Leticia?

**(c)** ¿Qué hará mañana?

**(d)** ¿Qué tiempo hace?

**(e)** ¿Dónde está el hotel?

**(f)** ¿Qué va a hacer el domingo por la mañana?

SAMPLE E

**Question 11**

Read Carlos' blog and answer the questions **in Spanish**.

¡Hola a todos! Ayer estuve en el mejor concierto del mundo. Fonsi tocó acá en Buenos Aires. Fue un concierto superguay; cantó todas las canciones de sus discos, pero lo más emocionante de todo fue que cuando empezó a tocar la canción "Échame la culpa", Demi Lovato apareció en el escenario cantando con él. Cantaron los dos a dúo y todo el mundo lloraba de emoción. Demi llevaba una minifalda negra y una camiseta también negra con reflejos dorados que le quedaba superbién. Iba muy guapa. El concierto terminó a la una de la mañana y yo llegué a casa cerca de las tres de la madrugada porque había mucha cola para salir. Llegué cansadísimo. El mejor concierto del mundo.

**(a)** ¿En qué ciudad tuvo lugar el concierto?

**(b)** ¿Qué llevaba Demi Lovato?

**(c)** ¿A qué hora terminó el concierto?

**(d)** ¿A qué hora llegó Carlos a casa?

**Question 12**

Read the following text and answer the questions **in English**.

# FESTIVAL INTERNACIONAL DE MÚSICA – BENICASSIM 2020

Entrada (un día) – cincuenta euros
Abono (cuatro días) – ciento cincuenta euros

- Hay transporte público cada media hora desde los aeropuertos de Valencia, Barcelona y Madrid
- Festival con quince grupos cada noche
- Campfest – se permite hacer camping cerca de la playa (necesitas tu tienda, un saco de dormir y una linterna)
- En el festival hay zonas de comida rápida, Wi-fi gratis, agua potable gratis
- No está permitido entrar con botellas de vidrio, paraguas, fuegos artificiales y barbacoas
- NO OLVIDES CREMA SOLAR, UN SOMBRERO Y PAPEL HIGIÉNICO

SAMPLE E

**(a)** What is the price of a four-day pass to the festival?

**(b)** How often does public transport run to the festival from the airports?

**(c)** Name **two** items that you need to bring with you if you are camping.

|  |
|---|
|  |
|  |

**(d)** Name **two** facilities that are available at the festival.

|  |
|---|
|  |
|  |

**(e)** Name **three** items that you cannot bring to the festival.

|  |
|---|
|  |
|  |
|  |

**(f)** Name **two** items that you should bring to the festival.

|  |
|---|
|  |
|  |

**Question 13**

Read the web page and answer the questions **in English**.

# CASA PACO

**Abierto de 13:00 a 17:00 y de 20:00 a 24:00**

| Menú del día 20€ | |
|---|---|
| **Primer plato:**<br>Sopa de cocido<br>Cazuela de pulpo<br>Mejillones | **Segundo plato:**<br>Brocheta de langostinos<br>Cocido<br>Mero a la plancha<br>**Postre o café** |

| Menú del día infantil 10€ | |
|---|---|
| **Primer plato:**<br>Sopa de verduras<br>Mini tapita de queso | **Segundo plato:**<br>Lagrimitas de pollo con patatas fritas<br>Espaguetis a la boloñesa<br>**Fruta o helado** |

- Las bebidas no están incluidas
- 5% en servicio a mesas
- Local climatizado
- Se aceptan tarjetas de crédito
- Prohibida la entrada de perros

**(a)** Name one dish that is listed as a starter on the menu of the day.

**(b)** How much is the children's menu?

SAMPLE E

**(c)** Name one main course on the children's menu.

**(d)** What are the dessert options on the children's menu?

**(e)** Drinks are included in the menus

True ☐ False ☐

**(f)** What is forbidden from entering the restaurant?

**Question 14**

Read the text and answer the questions **in English**.

## Amigos de los Mayores

Un grupo de jóvenes ha creado la asociación Amigos de los Mayores para ayudar a las personas mayores que viven solas. Alrededor de un 10% de los españoles mayores de setenta años vive solo sin ningún miembro de la familia, por lo que se sienten solos y sin compañía. Los jóvenes van a casa de los mayores una vez a la semana para ir a la compra con ellos, llevarlos al médico o salir a pasear. De esta manera, los ancianos hablan de su vida y recuerdos; a veces juegan al ajedrez, a las damas o al parchís. Los jóvenes hablan de los problemas actuales o les enseñan aplicaciones de móviles o nuevas tecnologías. "Lo importante es hablar, relacionarnos, que intercambiemos experiencias y conocimientos", han declarado. Doña Rosa, una señora de setenta y tres años, ha dicho: "Espero con mucha ilusión los martes, que es cuando viene Raúl", su acompañante, "porque así salgo a pasear y él me cuenta qué tal le ha ido la semana".

**(a)** Why did a group of young people set up *Amigos de los Mayores*?

**(b)** What does the figure 10% refer to?

**(c)** Name **three** things that the young people do with the elderly people.

**(d)** How old is Doña Rosa?

**(e)** Why does Doña Rosa look forward to Tuesdays?

SAMPLE E

**Question 15**

Read the text and answer the questions **in English**.

## Noviembre: Un mes para recordar a los muertos

**1.** En Irlanda la noche del 31 de octubre es una gran fiesta donde los niños disfrazados salen a la calle con bolsas y llaman a las puertas de los vecinos para pedir caramelos. Cuando un vecino abre la puerta, lo primero que hay que preguntar es "¿truco o trato?" para poder conseguir chocolatinas, chucherías o frutos secos. A veces también se pueden encontrar dulces caseros pequeños como magdalenas, o alguna fruta como mandarinas. El 1 de noviembre en Irlanda y también en otros países se celebra el Día de Todos los Santos y el 2 de noviembre el Día de los Difuntos. En estos días se recuerda a aquellos miembros de la familia que han fallecido y se reza por ellos.

**2.** En México en particular, este día se conoce con el nombre de Día de Muertos, una fiesta que tiene sus orígenes en la mezcla entre la religión de los pueblos indígenas y la religión católica. Los mexicanos creen que las personas que mueren están con nosotros pero de otra manera, y que en ese día vuelven para no ser olvidados. Es una fiesta de esperanza y alegría. Los mexicanos van a las tumbas de sus familiares, donde ponen muchas velas y llevan la comida y la bebida que le gustaba a la persona muerta. También colocan un pan especial: el pan de muertos, que es un pan dulce cubierto de azúcar; y una flor amarilla que tiene un fuerte olor. Es característico el disfraz de los muertos; los vestidos de las mujeres son de alegres colores muy vivos que contrastan con su maquillaje: la cara pintada entera de blanco representando una calavera.

**3.** Hoy en día esta fiesta es muy conocida no sólo en México sino también en países como Estados Unidos o Suecia, donde ese día hay desfiles de niños con sus padres y jóvenes, que disfrazados como calaveras, recorren las calles de sus ciudades.

**(a)** What Irish celebration is described in the first paragraph? (paragraph 1)

**(b)** Name **three** food items that children receive. (paragraph 1)

**(c)** What is the date of *el Día de Todos los Santos*? (paragraph 1)

**(d)** Name **two** things that people in Mexico bring to the tombs of their deceased relatives. (paragraph 2)

**(e)** What exactly is *pan de muertos*? (paragraph 2)

**(f)** Name **one** country, other than Mexico, that celebrates *el Día de Muertos*. (paragraph 3)

SAMPLE E

| **Section C** | **Writing** | **80 marks** |
|---|---|---|

**Question 16**

James is going on a trip to Malaga. Fill in the form **in Spanish** using the details below.

James O'Brien lives at 129 Foxhill Lane, Ashfield, Dublin 13 and his date of birth is 14 January 1990. He is booking a flight from Dublin to Malaga on 21 July at 10:30 am. He is paying by credit card and his email address is jamobri@mailer.com. His mobile number is 086 9814 604.

IBERIA

**DETALLES DEL VIAJE**

**Destino:** ____________________

**Salida desde:** ____________________

**Hora del vuelo:** ____________________

**DETALLES DEL PASAJERO**

**Nombre:** ____________________

**Apellido:** ____________________

**Hombre/Mujer:** ____________________

**Fecha de nacimiento:** ____________________

**Dirección:** ____________________

**Número de teléfono:** ____________________

**Correo electrónico:** ____________________

**Forma de pago:** Cheque ☐

Tarjeta de crédito ☐

**Question 17**

You decide to put a photo on Instagram for your Spanish friends. Write **five** complete sentences **in Spanish** to describe the photo.

| |
|---|
| |
| |
| |
| |
| |
| |
| |
| |

SAMPLE E

**Question 18**

Write a blog **in Spanish**. Answer **either (a) or (b)**.

| **(a)** Fuiste a un concierto de Ed Sheeran en Dublín anoche. Escribe un blog sobre el concierto.<br><br>Menciona:<br>• Cómo fuiste al concierto<br>• Qué hiciste en el concierto<br>• Tu opinión del concierto<br>• Por qué te gusta Ed Sheeran<br>• Otros cantantes o grupos que te gustan | **OR** | **(b)** Escribe un blog sobre tus pasatiempos.<br><br>Menciona:<br>• Las redes sociales<br>• La televisión<br>• Los deportes<br>• La música<br>• Salir con tus amigos |
|---|---|---|

Junior Cycle Final Examination
Sample Paper F

# Spanish

## Common Level

Time: 2 hours

360 marks

| Examination number | | | | |
|---|---|---|---|---|
| | | | | |

SAMPLE F

## Instructions

There are **three** sections in this paper.

| | | | |
|---|---|---|---|
| Section A | Listening | 140 marks | 8 questions |
| Section B | Reading | 140 marks | 7 questions |
| Section C | Writing | 80 marks | 3 questions |

Answer **all** questions.

Read the instructions carefully regarding the language to be used when answering the questions.

Write your answers in the spaces provided in this booklet.

| Section A | Listening | 140 marks |
|---|---|---|

## Question 1

Listen to the voice message and answer the questions **in Spanish**.

**(a)** ¿Por qué cancela la dentista la cita?

**(b)** ¿Cuándo es la nueva cita con la dentista?

| DÍA | FECHA | HORA |
|---|---|---|
| | | |

**(c)** Completa el número de teléfono:

98 __ __ __ 3__ __9

SAMPLE F

**Question 2**

Listen to the announcement at the supermarket and answer the questions below **in Spanish**.

**(a)** ¿Qué estación del año es?

**(b)** La fruta cuesta:

| | |
|---|---|
| 2 € por 50 gramos | ☐ |
| 2 € por 500 gramos | ☐ |
| 12 € por 50 gramos | ☐ |
| 12 € por 500 gramos | ☐ |

**(c)** ¿Cuándo empiezan las ofertas en heladería?

**Question 3**

Listen to the announcement at the airport and answer the questions **in Spanish**.

**(a)** ¿Cuál es el número del vuelo?

- EB136 ☐
- IB136 ☐
- EB137 ☐
- IB137 ☐

**(b)** El vuelo sale para:

- Barcelona ☐
- Bilbao ☐
- Bogotá ☐
- Bolivia ☐

**(c)** ¿De qué puerta de embarque sale?

**Question 4**

Listen to the advertisement and answer the questions below **in Spanish**.

**(a)** ¿Cuántos años de experiencia tiene la compañía ALSA?

5 ☐

100 ☐

105 ☐

**(b)** ¿De qué terminal del aeropuerto salen los autobuses?

Terminal 3 ☐

Terminal 4 ☐

Terminal 5 ☐

**(c)** ¿Cuántas salidas hay al día?

**(d)** ¿Cuánto tiempo tarda el autobús exprés?

4 horas y 40 minutos ☐

4 horas y 45 minutos ☐

5 horas y 40 minutos ☐

**Question 5**

Listen to the advertisement and answer the questions **in English**.

**(a)** When will the concert take place?

| Day | Date | Month |
| --- | --- | --- |
| | | |

**(b)** Name **four** Spanish cities where concerts will be held.

**(c)** Where can you buy tickets to the concert?

**(d)** What is *Sin ti*?

- a song ☐
- an album ☐
- a movie ☐
- a radio station ☐

SAMPLE F

**Question 6**

Listen to the voice messages. For each message write down **in English** the reason for calling, as in the example below.

| SPEAKER | REASON FOR CALLING |
|---|---|
| **(a)** Mamá | To tell her daughter to come home (because her grandparents are coming to visit). |
| **(b)** Irene | |
| **(c)** Josema | |
| **(d)** Sandra | |
| **(e)** Gustavo | |
| **(f)** Laura | |

## Question 7

Listen to Daniela describe a trip and answer the questions **in English**.

**(a)** When did Daniela travel to Barcelona with her classmates?

**(b)** In what year did construction of the *Sagrada Familia* cathedral start?

**(c)** What did the group do at *Las Ramblas*?

**(d)** What is *Port Aventura*?

- a shopping centre ☐
- a theme park ☐
- a beach ☐
- a sports centre ☐

SAMPLE F

**Question 8**

Listen to the **five** short conversations and put a tick (✓) in the correct box after each statement.

| | True | False | Not Mentioned |
|---|---|---|---|
| **(a)** The boy orders chicken and chips. | | | |
| **(b)** The book will be available on the $26^{th}$. | | | |
| **(c)** The boy has training until 7:30 pm. | | | |
| **(d)** The students are in maths class. | | | |
| **(e)** The man wants to download Spotify. | | | |

## Section B — Reading — 140 marks

**Question 9**

Match the following words and images by filling in the grid.

| | |
|---|---|
| **A. La joyería** | **1.** 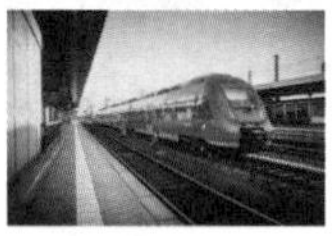 |
| **B. Zona peatonal** | **2.** 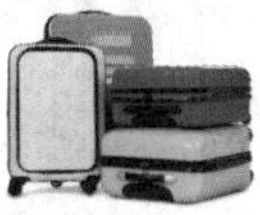 |
| **C. Carril de bicicletas** | **3.** 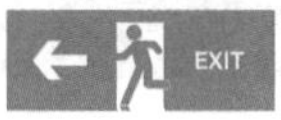 |
| **D. RENFE** | **4.** 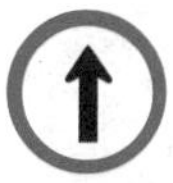 |
| **E. La piscina** | **5.** 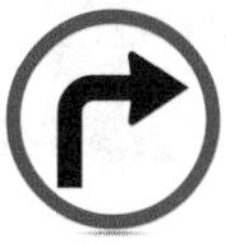 |
| **F. Equipaje** | **6.** 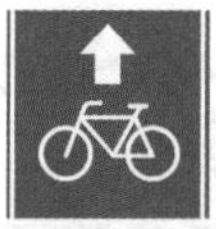 |
| **G. Salida** | **7.** 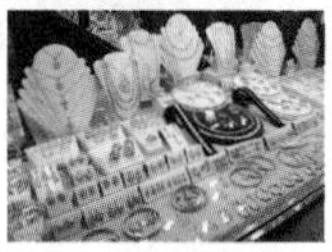 |
| **H. Todo recto** | **8.** 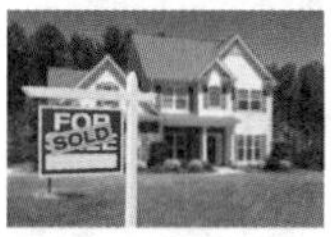 |
| **I. Gire a la derecha** | **9.** 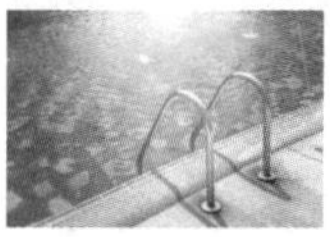 |
| **J. Se vende** | **10.** 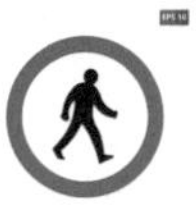 |

| LETRA | NÚMERO |
|---|---|
| A. | |
| B. | |
| C. | |
| D. | |
| E. | |
| F. | |
| G. | |
| H. | |
| I. | |
| J. | 8 |

**Question 10**

Match the texts below with the correct theme in the grid.

**A.**

**Grupo El loco**
Día: martes 23 a las 23:00
Puertas abiertas a partir de las 22:00
Lugar: Sala El Palenque
Precio: 30€

**B.**

Lavar con colores oscuros
Puede desteñir
Lavar con agua fría
Algodón 100%

**C.**

**Sala de arte**
Exposición: El arte medieval
Abierto: de 19 a 22
Importe: 5€

**D.**

Buscamos enfermeras con experiencia para trabajar en Italia
Ofrecemos buen salario, buenas condiciones de trabajo
Interesados mandar el cv a contrata@enfermeria.es

**E.**

**Transportes del Sur**
Almería-Granada (directo)
Tarifa: 15€
Salida: 06:30
Llegada: 08:15
Dársena: 7

F.

**Servicio de traducción e interpretación**

Traducciones juradas

c/Vigo 98

G.

**Película Los invencibles**

Sesión: 20:30

Fila: 14

Butaca: 54

Precio: 7€

H.

**Técnico de aire acondicionado**

Reparamos todas las marcas de aire acondicionado

Experiencia profesional

Llámanos al 956 79809

Todas las áreas cubiertas

| Letra | Tema |
|---|---|
| | A cinema ticket |
| C | A ticket for an art gallery |
| | A translator |
| | A clothes label |
| | A bus ticket |
| | Air conditioning repair service |
| | A concert ticket |
| | A job advertisement |

**Question 11**

Read Yusuf's blog and answer the questions **in Spanish.**

¡Hola! ¡Bienvenidos al blog de Yusuf! Hoy quiero hablaros de comida. A mí me gusta comer y cocinar platos nuevos. Creo que me parezco a mis padres porque a ellos les encanta cocinar para toda la familia. Mis abuelos, mis primos y tíos vienen algunos fines de semana y nos pasamos horas en la cocina. Cuando no hace mucho calor, comemos fuera en el patio y alguna vez hemos hecho barbacoa, pero no es lo normal. Un plato que me gusta mucho es la ensaladilla rusa. ¿La habéis probado? Es una ensalada de mayonesa. Tenéis que hervir patatas, zanahorias, guisantes y dos huevos. Luego lo cortáis todo en trocitos y añadís atún y la mayonesa. Cuando se mezcla todo, hay que ponerlo en el frigorífico porque tiene que estar frío. Se come frío y es perfecto en verano para combatir el calor. Escribidme si lo preparáis y decidme qué os parece. ¡Hasta luego!

**(a)** ¿Qué hace la familia de Yusuf cuando no hace mucho calor?

**(b)** ¿Qué es la ensaladilla rusa?

**(c)** ¿Cuáles son los ingredientes de la ensaladilla rusa?

**(d)** Es perfecto comer la ensaladilla rusa en verano

Verdadero ☐

Falso ☐

**Question 12**

Read the text and answer the questions **in English**.

# HOTEL ISLA CRISTINA

¡Bienvenidos a nuestro hotel!

Aquí podrás encontrar información sobre nuestras actividades de entretenimiento para esta semana:

**TopCocinero:**

- ¿Quieres aprender a cocinar platos sabrosos? Comida sana y natural para niños de ocho a doce años. Aprenderás trucos de gastronomía mediterránea.
- Lunes, miércoles y viernes de 17 a 19.
- Tarifa: 10€. Sala 7. Planta primera.

**Escape:**

- ¡Reúne a un grupo y a jugar! El grupo se encerrará en una habitación con un enigma para resolver.
- De jueves a domingo a las 12,30.
- Recomendado para grupos de entre 2 y 6 personas, a partir de 15 años.
- Tarifa: 50€ por grupo. Sala 05. Planta primera.

**Pista de patinaje sobre hielo:**

- Prueba nuestra pista de patinaje.
- Puedes conseguir tus patines allí mismo.
- Tarifa: 3€ por media hora de patinaje. Planta baja.

SAMPLE F

**Acceso al gimnasio y clases:**

- Puedes acceder a nuestras instalaciones y disfrutar de nuestras clases virtuales dirigidas por un monitor.
- De lunes a viernes de 7 a 23 y sábados y domingos de 8 a 21.
- Sólo para adultos.
- Tarifa: 5€ todo el día.

**(a)** What age group is the TopChef workshop for?

**(b)** On what **three** days of the week will the TopChef workshop take place?

**(c)** When can you do the Escape Room challenge?

**(d)** On what floor of the hotel will the Escape Room challenge take place?

**(e)** On what floor of the hotel can you find the ice skating rink?

**(f)** Who are the gym classes suitable for?

## Question 13

Read the TV listings and answer the questions **in English**.

| | | |
|---|---|---|
| Antena 3 | 12:15 | **Cocina abierta de Karlos Arguiñano**<br>Décima temporada de este programa en el que Karlos Arguiñano, el cocinero más famoso de la televisión, ofrece nuevas recetas. |
| TVE1 | 13:30 | **Corazón**<br>Crónica social sobre los famosos del mundo de la música, la moda, el cine y el teatro. Reportajes de las grandes pasarelas, los cantantes y actores de moda. |
| LaSexta | 16:30 | **Bob Esponja**<br>Bob Esponja esconde la fórmula secreta en su casa y debe protegerla de Plankton. Dibujo animado. |
| Teledeporte | 17:30 | **Mundial de Atletismo**<br>Los mejores atletas del mundo se dan cita en Doha, donde se disputa el Mundial entre el 27 de septiembre y el 6 de octubre. La delegación española intentará mejorar los pobres resultados de Londres. Kenia, Jamaica y Estados Unidos son los favoritos. |
| Telecinco | 18:20 | **Alaska, última frontera**<br>Realidad. Atz y su familia salen a cazar un oso pardo pero a su padre le entran los nervios. |
| LaSexta | 19:00 | **Noticias**<br>Informativo que presenta las noticias que han ocurrido a lo largo de la jornada. |
| Antena 3 | 23:30 | **Cine: El secreto de mi hija**<br>Suspense/Thriller. Una joven se ve implicada sin querer en el atraco de la joyería donde trabaja su madre. Película canadiense protagonizada por Jennifer Grant. |
| TVE2 | 00:45 | **China, los tesoros del Imperio de Jade**<br>Historia. En Xian, antigua capital de China, la terracota y el jade son testigos y narradores de la historia. |

**(a)** Who is Karlos Arguiñano?

**(b)** What type of programme is Bob Esponja?

**(c)** What sport is being shown at 5:30pm?

**(d)** What time is the movie being shown?

SAMPLE F

**Question 14**

Read the following three profiles and answer the questions **in English**.

**Marcos**

Me llamo Marcos y estoy estudiando Empresariales en la Universidad Complutense de Madrid. Trabajo como camarero los fines de semana y voy a clases durante la semana. El sueldo de camarero no es muy bueno pero me ayuda para mis gastos. Lo que más me gusta son las propinas. Este verano quiero comprarme una moto con mis ahorros así que no me iré de vacaciones.

**Rosaura**

¡Hola! Me llamo Rosaura y quiero estudiar Derecho. Quiero ser abogada para cambiar el mundo. Me preocupa el medioambiente porque si no cuidamos la naturaleza nos vamos a quedar sin un lugar donde vivir. Soy voluntaria en Greenpeace y nos dedicamos a limpiar zonas que están sucias o contaminadas. Por ejemplo, el fin de semana pasado estuvimos en la playa recogiendo botellas de plástico, bolsas y restos de picnics y comida. Por favor, recordad no dejar basura en la playa. Recoged lo que habéis comido, podéis tirarlo en las papeleras y cubos de basura que hay a la salida de la playa.

**Bruno**

¡Hola! Me llamo Bruno y soy fontanero. Soy autónomo y tengo mi propio negocio. En mi tiempo libre me gusta ir a conciertos. La semana que viene voy al Festival de Música de Benidorm, donde voy a tocar con mi banda Los Rocanrroleros. Toco el bajo en la banda. Normalmente ensayamos los jueves por la noche después del trabajo. Estoy pensando en dar clases de bajo y de guitarra porque soy muy bueno y he conocido a varias personas que quieren aprender.

**(a)** What is Marcos' part time job?

**(b)** What is he going to do with his savings?

**(c)** What would Rosaura like to be in the future?

**(d)** What did she do last weekend?

**(e)** When is Bruno going to the music festical?

**(f)** When does Bruno rehearse with his band?

**Question 15**

Read the leaflet and answer the questions **in English**.

# ¡TODOS RUMBO A BARCELONA!

La cadena de hoteles CINCO ESTRELLAS le regala la promoción "Fin de semana en Barcelona" donde encontrará lo siguiente:

- Descuentos para los distintos museos, parques de atracciones y puntos turísticos de la ciudad (incluida la Casa Batlló, pero no la Sagrada Familia)
- Un bonobús que podrá usar en todas las líneas de autobús de la ciudad válido para dos días
- Una guía de la ciudad
- 20% de descuento en todos los departamentos de El Corte Inglés (excepto en perfumería)
- Precios especiales en nuestros restaurantes socios. Busque la lista de restaurantes en nuestra página web que se actualiza todas las semanas

NO lo dude y haga su reserva en alguno de nuestros hoteles para poder disfrutar de esta magnífica promoción que será sin duda un ahorro en sus vacaciones.

Teléfono gratuito: 657 008 009

**(a)** Name **two** kinds of tourist attraction offering discounted entry as part of this promotion.

| |
|---|
| |
| |

**(b)** Which famous tourist attraction is not offering discounted entry with this promotion?

| |
|---|
| |

**(c)** On what form of public transport can the travel pass be used? Tick (✓) the correct answer.

| | |
|---|---|
| metro | ☐ |
| bus | ☐ |
| both metro and bus | ☐ |

**(d)** For how long is the travel pass valid?

| |
|---|
| |

**(e)** Which department of *El Corte Inglés* is not offering a 20% discount?

| |
|---|
| |

**(f)** Where can you find the list of restaurants offering special prices?

| |
|---|
| |

SAMPLE F

| Section C | Writing | 80 marks |
|---|---|---|

**Question 16**

Your Spanish teacher is organising an exchange to Valladolid and you want to take part in the exchange. Fill in the form below **in Spanish**.

| | |
|---|---|
| **Nombre:** | |
| **Apellido:** | |
| **Fecha de nacimiento:** | |
| **Edad:** | |

**Describe tu familia:**

**Describe tu casa:**

**Question 17**

Read the text messages between Miguel and Laura. Use all the spaces to continue the conversation **in Spanish**.

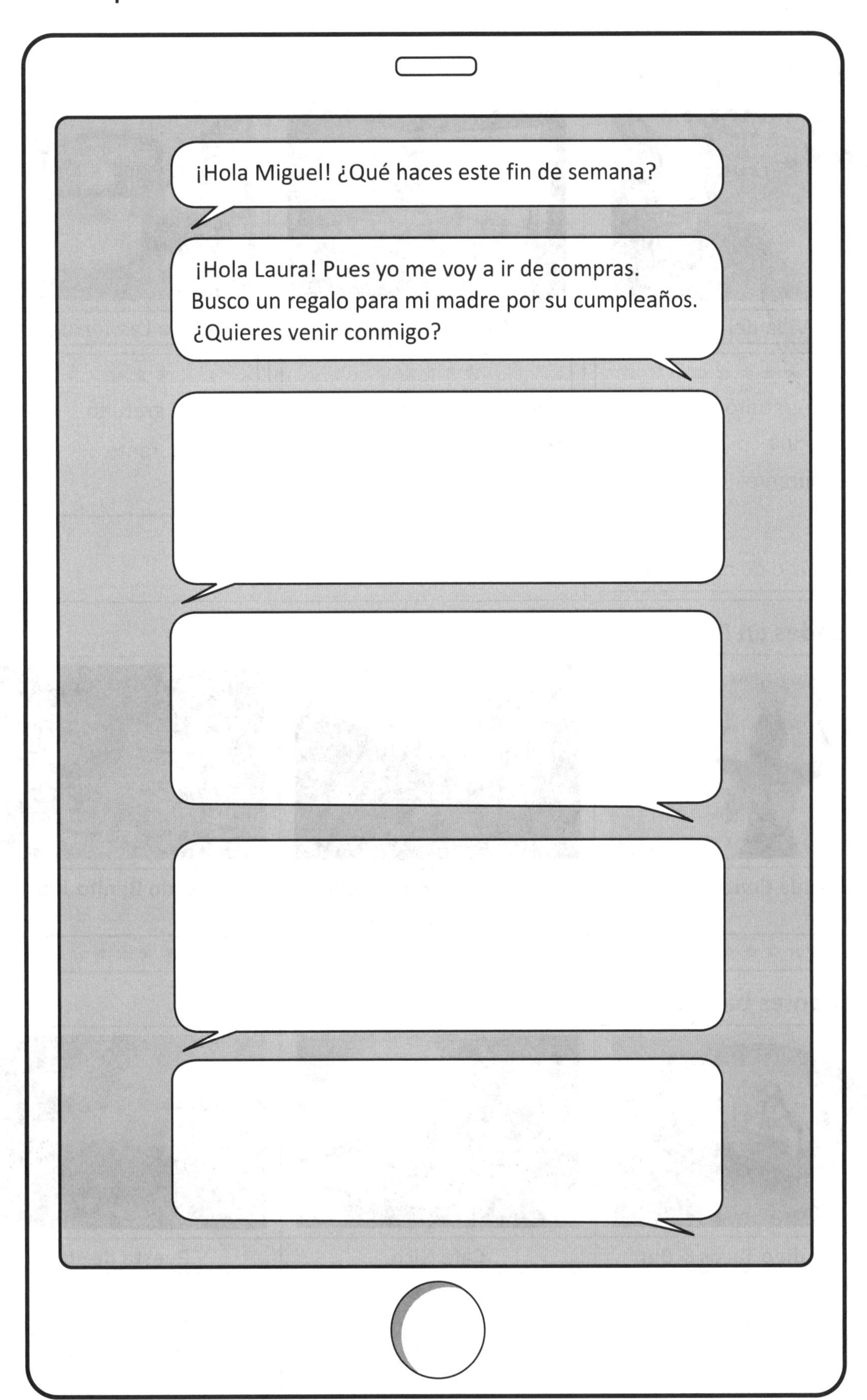


SAMPLE F

## Question 18

Read about the Mexican town of Puerto Escondido. Imagine you are spending a holiday there and write a blog **in Spanish** about your experience. Use some of the information in the texts below in your answer.

### Hostales en Puerto Escondido

|  |  |  |
|---|---|---|
| **Villa del Mar** | **Hotel Panorama** | **Casa Las Tortugas** |
| ★★★★☆<br> Wifi gratuito<br> Piscina<br>Restaurante<br> Bar<br>Servicio de habitaciones | ★★½☆☆<br> Oferta especial<br> Wifi | ★★★☆☆<br>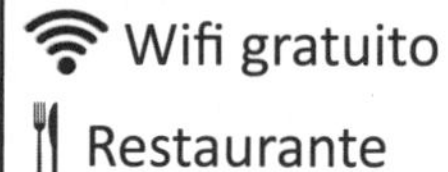 Wifi gratuito<br>Restaurante<br>Bar |

### Actividades en Puerto Escondido

|  |  |  |
|---|---|---|
| **Tienda Central Surf** | **Tour nocturno por la laguna de Manialtepec** | **Mercado Benito Juárez** |
| ★★★★☆ | ★★★☆☆ | ★★★★½ |

### Restaurantes baratos

|  |  |  |
|---|---|---|
| **Escondido Tacos & Bar** | **Café Nico** | **Puesta de sol** |
| ★★☆☆☆<br>Comida mexicana<br>Cócteles | ★★★★☆<br>Comida libanesa<br>Saludable | ★★★★★<br>Restaurante italiano<br>Pizza, pasta |